Winning

School Board Elections

With an Anti-Wokeness Platform

How to Create and Run a Successful "Stop Wokeness in K12 Schools Campaign"

By

Corey Lee Wilson

Winning School Board Elections

Winning School Board Elections With an Anti-Wokeness Platform

Fratire Publishing books can be purchased in bulk with special discounts for educational purposes, organizational gifts, sales promotions, and special editions can be created to specifications. All inquiries for such can be made below.

FRATIRE PUBLISHING LLC
4533 Temescal Canyon Rd. # 308
Corona, CA 92883
www.FratirePublishing.com
FratirePublishing@att.net
(951) 638-5502

FratirePublishing
Relevant Books for **SAPIENT** Beings

Fratire Publishing is all about common sense and relevant books for sapient beings. If this sounds like you and you can never have enough common sense, wisdom and relevancy, then visit us at www.FratirePublishing.com.

Printed paperback and eBook ePUB by Ingram Spark in La Vergne, Tennessee, USA
Copyright © 2023: October 2023
ISBN 978-1-953319-26-5 (Paperback)
ISBN 978-1-953319-39-5 (eBook)
WSBE-01-PDF (pdf)
WSBE-01-EPUB (epub)
LCCN 2023919556

Book cover logo by dasignlady at:
https://www.redbubble.com/people/dasignlady/shop?artistUserName=dasignlady&iaCode=all-stickers.

Winning School Board Elections

Contents

Acknowledgements

Below are the major contributors to *Winning School Board Elections With an Anti-Wokeness Platform* that were borrowed from, verbatim, quoted, and conceptualized, from a little to a lot. Wherever this happened, their contributions and sources are acknowledged in the Resources section at the end of the book, as well as the Index section, and done intentionally so as to not distract the reader from the themes and messages covered throughout the chapters of the handbook.

Ron DeSantis – In America, Florida Governor DeSantis is the leading and most vocal anti-woke politician and rising star of conservatives. DeSantis sided with parents during the pandemic, when he made the difficult decision to force school districts to reopen, over the objections of unions, many health officials, and the national media. As the pandemic subsided, and the debates over curricular issues emerged, the governor led the nations by passing an aggressive slate of bills addressing everything from CRT and gender ideology to viewpoint diversity, civics education, parental rights, and took on Disney's woke agenda, bringing all of these issues to the national spotlight.

Christopher F. Rufo – Is an American conservative activist, contributing editor of *City Journal,* New College of Florida board member, senior fellow at the Manhattan Institute for Policy Research, and leading the fight against Progressivism madness in American institutions. He is a vocal opponent of critical race theory, former documentary filmmaker and fellow at the Discovery Institute, the Claremont Institute, The Heritage Foundation, and the Foundation Against Intolerance and Racism. In 2022, he earned a Master of Liberal Arts in Extension Studies from Harvard Extension School.

Moms for Liberty – Is the United States' leading parental rights organization and is dedicated to fighting for the survival of America by unifying, educating, and empowering parents to defend their parental rights at all levels of government. The educational non-profit 501 (c) 4 has over 250 chapters in 42 states in America as of October 2023, and activates liberty-minded leaders to serve in elected positions. Their members understand school board races are some of the most important elections on the ballot, and therefore, seek to provide school board candidates with the resources, such as their Campaign Kit, to successfully run for office.

The Heritage Foundation – Is an American conservative think tank that is primarily geared toward public policy and the foundation took a leading role in the conservative movement during the presidency of Ronald Reagan, whose policies were taken from Heritage's policy study Mandate for Leadership. The Heritage Foundation has partnered with congruent organizations to provide various model legislation, including their own, that states can use to protect education freedom. Their Save Our Schools Parental Rights Resources are extensive with instructional, legislative, and school board training resources.

S.A.P.I.E.N.T. Being – The Society Advancing Personal Intelligence and Enlightenment Now Together (S.A.P.I.E.N.T.) Being is the leading anti-woke and anti-progressivism madness organization and think tank in the USA. They publish *Education Madness: A SAPIENT Being's Guide to Fixing America's Dysfunctional & Illiberal Educational Systems*, a textbook from their Sapient Conservative Textbook (SCT) Program, an alternative social studies textbooks program to counter woke and progressive madness in America's educational institutions, and help return conservative values, viewpoint diversity, and sapience to high school and college campuses.

A Parental Rights Introduction

Parents across America have stepped up to run for their local school board and that's great news!

Many of these parents sprang into action in response to extreme COVID mandates in America's public schools as well as radical gender and race-based curricula pushed by the state's teachers' unions. Parents and parent groups are calling for greater transparency from school districts and school boards, on everything from school budgets and teacher training curricula to what is being taught in the classroom.

District school boards and county Boards of Education in California typically consist of 5 or 7 seats, with each seat being either "at-large" or representing a "trustee area." The boundaries of a trustee area might change according to each census to keep them equal in population. Depending on your district, there will usually be 1-4 seats up for election at a time since school board elections are regularly staggered.

Is it possible for you to be a member of your local school board? Yes it is! School board seats are locally elected public offices. To win a seat on a school board, you'll need to run a campaign and win the election. For a complete guide and strategy to accomplish this, please check out Chapter 10-The Moms for Liberty School Board Candidate Playbook & More.

While school boards are a quintessential example of representative democracy, you may be surprised to know that many districts experience low participation by both candidates and voters. The National School Boards Association's (NSBA) Center for Public Education examines the data behind uncontested elections and low voter turnout.

The nation's nearly 14,000 school boards are responsible for overseeing and managing the educational resources that serve 56.6 million students across the nation. "The decisions made by school boards affect virtually every important aspect of local schools, from boundaries to bus schedules, curriculum to clubs, funding to field trips," according to the New York State School Boards Association.

Most school boards are put together through elections while a smaller number are appointed. However, whether elected or appointed, these public officials take on one of the most demanding roles in America, namely, the leadership of public schools and the education of the children in their local community.

It is clear, then, that participating in the election of boards of education is of paramount importance, but the data show a very different picture, with very low participation by both candidates and voters.

To help address these challenges, new right-leaning political action committees are pouring money into school board races, aiming to flip control of who governs schools in a way that rivals the role that teachers unions have historically had in these contests.

For much less than what it would cost them to influence a seat in the House or Senate, these PACs are putting thousands of dollars at a time— sometimes just hundreds—into races for local school boards and as a result, changing education on a national scale.

Lack of Candidates

A 2014 Gallup Poll shows that 56 percent of Americans believe that local school boards, rather than state or federal government, should have the greatest influence on what is taught in public schools. However, school board elections often find themselves with uncontested candidates and empty school board seats. According to Ballotpedia, the candidates per seat ratio was 1.89 in 2014, 1.72 in 2015, and 1.90 in 2016 school board elections.

Researchers point out that uncontested candidates and empty school board seats have become an issue in school board elections. For example:

- In New Jersey, there was a total of 805 uncontested school board seats, and for 130 of them, no one was even on the ballot in 2015.

- In Virginia, an entire county had no contested school board seats, and two districts didn't have a single individual running in 2015.

- In California, in 2015, one county had eight open seats from 25 school boards, but no single candidate signed up to run, and existing boards had to appoint members to fill these openings.

Low Voter Turnout

Voter turnout for political office elections has gone up since 2014, according to the U.S. Census Bureau. However, in local school board elections, voter turnout has been discouragingly low—often just 5 percent or 10 percent. According to local news:

- Only 8.7 percent of eligible Los Angeles County voters participated in the 2019 local school board election;

- In a school district in Iowa, 498 voters—10.05 percent of registered voters—decided the 2017 race for school board members;

- In South Dakota, in a school district with 2,054 voters at the time of the election, only 245 (12 percent) participated in the local school board election.

Let Your Voice Be Heard

While factors such as the timing of elections, demographic change, and voters' lack of awareness of candidates can affect school board elections, uncontested candidates and low voter turnout remain serious concerns in terms of selecting board members who can truly represent the local community to make school policies.

Research shows that school board elections with relatively higher voter turnout and a broader range of constituents (e.g., holding school board elections at the same time as state- or national-level elections) are associated with higher academic performance of students, as opposed to elections with lower voter turnout.

With that said, are you up to becoming a school board member and inspired enough to make a change for the better, for your children, your school district, your country?

If the answer is yes, this *Winning School Board Elections With an Anti-Wokeness Platform* guidebook is going to be the right decision for you. In it you will find most everything you need to know about school board candidacy, platform topics, and elections, as well as useful links for more information.

If not immediately running for a school board position, and your viewpoint is more of a concerned parent or parent's rights group, this handbook is also for you, and Chapter 9-Stopping America's Impending Destruction From Woke Madness might be of more interest to you.

So, what are you waiting for? You're not alone on this journey—and in great company with like-minded partners to help you succeed. Now is the time to get started. Use this handy guidebook as a resource and the best of success to you with your "Stop Wokeness in K12 Schools Campaign."

1 – How Woke Are America's Schools?

Credit: EAG.

Learning has been replaced by an aggressive political agenda designed to instill doubt, mental pain, and low expectations in students. According to government statistics, America's education system is failing. According to one expert, lower expectations and the shift in focus from academic excellence in mathematics, science, reading, and history toward the implementation of social constructs like critical race theory equals fewer literate graduates.

As noted by Thomas Sowell, a senior fellow at the Hoover Institution, Stanford University, decades of dumbed-down education no doubt have something to do with this, but there is more to it than that. Education is not merely neglected in many of our schools today, but is replaced to a great extent by ideological indoctrination. Moreover, it is largely indoctrination based on the same set of underlying and unexamined assumptions among teachers and institutions.

If our educational institutions—from the schools to the universities—were as interested in a "diversity of ideas" as they are obsessed with racial diversity, students would at least gain experience in seeing the assumptions behind different visions and the role of logic and evidence in debating those differences.

The failure of our educational system goes beyond what they fail to teach. It includes what they do teach, or rather indoctrinate, and the graduates they send out into the world, incapable of seriously weighing alternatives for themselves or for American society.

"Public records and other evidence show that state-level and some local education officials are no longer focused on maintaining high academic standards and providing the best public education possible to students," Liv Finne wrote in her September 2021 report regarding the lowering of academic standards by school officials in Washington state as they implement CRT.

"Instead, a concern for learning has been replaced by an aggressive political agenda designed to instill doubt, mental pain and low expectations in students. This race-centered agenda also seeks to divide children from teachers, their own communities and from each other. This harmful trend can only be resolved through policies that return high-quality academic standards to public education and well-funded and supportive education-choice programs that allow families to access alternatives services to meet the learning needs of all children."

Statistics Show America's Education System is Failing

Liv Finne, a former adjunct scholar now serving as Director of the Center for Education at Washington Policy Center, has been analyzing education policy for the past 13 years. Her research suggests the unmistakable decline in the literacy of America's students from fourth to twelfth grade is a direct result of the shift from academic excellence toward social constructs such as CRT.

"Internationally, we do pretty well at the fourth grade," Finne told the *Epoch Times*, "but we decline from there." Recent statistics support her claim.

Government data for 2019 shows the average fourth grader has a 41 percent proficiency level in mathematics. By the eighth grade, the proficiency level drops to 34 percent. By the twelfth grade, America's students have an average math proficiency level of only 24 percent. In reading, fourth graders have an average proficiency rate of 35 percent. By eighth grade, the proficiency level drops to 34 percent, and by the twelfth grade, America's average student shows only a slight proficiency improvement to 37 percent. In writing, the proficiency levels are 28 percent in fourth grade with eighth and twelfth graders sharing a score of 27 percent.

America's students fare worse in science, with fourth-graders having only a 36 percent proficiency rate and eighth-graders dropping to 35 percent. Twelfth-graders have only a 22 rate of proficiency in science. The worst scores come in history, with fourth-graders starting out with only 20 percent proficiency and dropping to 15 percent by the eighth grade. By grade 12, America's students have a paltry 12 percent proficiency level in history.

Recent numbers from USA Facts show similar results. According to Finne, there are a number of reasons for the steady decline in literacy among America's students the longer they remain in school. Number one is "the low expectations we have of our teachers."

Lowering the Academic Achievement Bar

Rather than develop curriculum that provides students with the qualifications needed to graduate high school, Liv Finne says the education system has opted to lower the bar of academic standards.

"They're lowering the bar in a couple of ways," Finne explained. "Like the Ethnic Studies framework passed by the State of Washington in 2019, critical race theory concepts are now woven into the learning standards of all of the different subjects."

As Finne explains, traditional educational standards have been reorganized into systems of oppression and the whole CRT construct—a "false philosophy from radical professors in higher education" is now being "imposed as the truth" in the standards of learning in K-12 schools.

"When you take attention away from the basics, and focus on teaching this ideology, you're going to get a lowered level of knowledge and skill acquisition of the basics in reading, math, history, and science; not to mention learning falsehoods in history like the 1619 Project," Finne insisted. "It's astonishing."

The Status Quo System

According to Liv Finne, the new push by the school system to abandon efforts of academic achievement and shift toward social constructs like CRT is an effort to hide the fact that they have failed in their jobs to educate our children.

"The whole idea is that if the community knew that their schools are not educating their children to basic levels they would rise up," Finne said. "Just look what's happening now with the uprising of parents against CRT in places like Loudoun County [Virginia] and they're still going forward with it. It's a huge uphill battle for parents."

"The whole system has promoted children whether they learn the content or not," Finne said. "So why should they care if a whole generation of children lost the content of a year (from the pandemic)? It's consistent with their practice. They do not individualize education. They don't make sure each individual child is ready to go on to the next grade. They move them along, especially minority children. The only people blocking real reform are the defenders of the status quo, the ones who like it just the way it is."

Teachers Unions are indeed the ones who fight against charter schools, school choice, and parental involvement and fought to keep kids out of classrooms during the COVID-19 outbreak. According to Finne, "if they really cared about black lives, they would be expanding their options for charter schools. But they're not. If these critical race theorists are truly intent on helping the children, they would be going after the unions. But they're not."

The Silver COVID-19 Lining

Ironically, Liv Finne believes the greatest hope for the education of America's children will rise from the ashes of the COVID-19 school lockdowns.

"The silver lining is we will eventually figure out how terrible it has been," Finne said. "Through the COVID shutdowns it has become clear how far behind so many kids are and the movements to expand school choice is not going away, because parents have woken up. That's what's so exciting about the COVID school shutdowns. Together with the takeover of the schools by this crazy critical race theory idea that children are bad and if they're white they're racist and if they're not white they're victims, that is going to lead to lawsuits.

"Maybe out of the ashes of this, school choice will arise," Finne opined of the educational chaos that ensued during the lockdowns. "This is still a democracy. The exchange of ideas is still happening in education because we do care about our children. That's what I'm hoping; that people will see the wisdom of giving parents real control, not just window dressing like involving parents and having parent involvement coordinators, but real control."

National Suicide by Education

It's true that children are our future, for good or ill, depending on their education. Ill-educate children, as we are doing in the United States and Canada, and the result will be cultural decay, social breakdown, and political decline.

We now teach our children that our country is illegitimate, based on genocide and racism, and is systemically evil. Will this lead the next generation to love or despise their country? Who will volunteer for the military, to risk their lives to protect their evil country? When generals assert that the military is racist and sexist, homophobic and transphobic, and harbors white supremacists and domestic terrorists, who will volunteer for the military, to risk their lives to protect their country? Recruitment for the military in both the United States and Canada is severely down, and no one can figure out how to increase it.

We teach our children that our society is divided between helpless victims and cruel oppressors. BIPOC (black, indigenous, people of color) and females are all and everywhere oppressed, and whites and males, Christians and Jews, and (astonishingly) Asians are privileged, evil villains.

11

Children learn to fear and hate their fellow citizens of other races, sexes, religions, and ethnicities. What kind of society will we have when we teach children that race hatred, sexism, and ethno-supremacy are justified and virtuous?

Children are taught that speaking and writing correct English is racist, and so they must not learn correct English.

Math too is racist, when really, there are no correct answers, and to deny that two plus two can equal anything is oppressive. The demand for correct answers, logic, and scientific proof are sins of "whiteness" that must be eradicated from the socially just society. Thus, it isn't a weakness that American children perform poorly on international tests of reading, math, and science, but a demonstration of virtue, of social justice.

When schools teach the counterfactual lie that police every day murder innocent black and brown people, a lie refuted by every serious study, is it a surprise that police are viewed by black and brown children with fear and hatred? The constant insults and attacks on police by BIPOC children as well as adults are a predictable result of such inculcation.

So too is the low morale of police in almost all urban jurisdictions, their unwillingness to engage in proactive policing, the flood of resignations, early retirements, transfers to rural jurisdictions, and suicides, and the lack of recruits to fill the large gaps in almost every urban police force. It's no surprise that the crime rate has shot up in every urban jurisdiction.

Race and gender disparities in academic participation and performance are explained by one and only one possible factor: racist and sexist discrimination. The other likely causes—family weakness in single-parent homes, community pathologies, and individual choices—may not be mentioned or investigated. In this way, disparities in participation or performance are deemed illegitimate, and therefore must be wiped out in order to achieve "equity," that is, equal results among census categories of the population, and "social justice."

Thus, poor performers are "victims," and measures must be taken to ensure that outcomes are the same.

This is done by giving preferences to underperforming BIPOC pupils and students, canceling accelerated programs for which they do not qualify, canceling examinations in which they do poorly, and setting aside performance standards. Programs in which females are underrepresented must prioritize recruiting females through special preferences and benefits.

BIPOC pupils and students are taught that their academic participation and performance is not their responsibility, but the responsibility of others who victimize them, and who owe them preference, benefits, and reparations. This is the perfect pedagogical plan for destroying individual motivation and a sense of responsibility. There's always someone else to blame.

In order to advance "equity," based on demographic "representation" of race, sex, ethnicity, etc., alternative criteria for judgment, such as individual achievement, merit, and potential, are denounced as, you know, "racist," and rejected. So recruitment to academia, science, media, professions, and government will be of the demographically underrepresented, not of the most capable candidates.

The foundation of this plan is the racism of low expectations, assuming that people from BIPOC categories could never make it on merit. This guarantees mediocrity or complete incompetence throughout our institutions: in medical care, scholarship and teaching, engineering, the press, law, and governance. The consequent trajectory is a societal decline and decay.

Female pupils and students are taught that they are being excluded due to sexist discrimination.

This counterfactual claim ignores the reality that females are the majority in universities and in most schools and programs. Those few programs where they are not, in spite of all of the heavy recruiting—physical sciences, mathematics, computer science—is a result of the choices of females who prefer to enter other fields. Yet females are continually told that they are victims of sexist discrimination. And male pupils and students are told that non-existent female victimhood is their fault.

Given the understanding that reason, logic, the search for evidence and correct answers, and science are taught as features of oppressive "whiteness," it should come as no surprise that schools discourage students from basing their understandings on scientific facts. A particular focus of teaching from kindergarten through graduate studies is the rejection of biology and its knowledge of biological factors in human life. Biological sex is now taught to be irrelevant to human life; the only thing that counts is one's feelings about gender.

Children are taught that they can be any of a hundred genders that they choose. Some teachers groom children to be supporters and "allies" of LGBTQ+, and to join in wherever they choose. Some children who are uncomfortable with their sex or confused about it are in some schools recruited into the trans community. Schools funnel pupils to sex transition clinics run by people, who still call themselves doctors, where children are subjected to life-changing chemical treatments and surgical mutilation in the futile effort to transform children from their biological sex to a replica of the other.

What devious force brought all of this cultural destruction into being?

Who injected this destructive poison into our educational system? The source, of course, is our universities. They were taken over by grievance studies advanced by various particular interest groups. First and most decisive were the feminists who established women's and gender studies to advance what they defined as the narrow interests of women.

They adopted the Marxist model of society divided into two warring classes; in place of the proletariat versus the bourgeoisie, they defined the conflicting classes as females versus the patriarchy, all men. The feminists inspired queer studies and LGBTQ+ activism. Black studies, Latinx studies, and Asian studies all championed their races in alleged conflict with the other races. Universities no longer were about what can we learn about the world and its people, but about what you could do through propaganda and activism to advance the narrow interests of your category.

All of these activisms were absorbed in social science and humanities programs, often by joint appointed professors with one or another grievance study. Administrators were either activists themselves or were won over and instituted "social justice" measures of "diversity, equity, and inclusion," hiring "diversity officers" to police the staff and students to ensure that no "wrong think" was allowed to flourish.

Faculties of education, being weak in academic content and lax in pursuing that, adopted grievance theory with a vengeance, and trained their students, the future school administrators and teachers, in the most radical forms of grievance activism. The faculties of education have contaminated our K-12 schools and made them what they are now.

With an Anti-Wokeness Platform

2 – What is Progressivism & Who Are These So-Called Progressives?

Credit: Chad Crowe.

American leftists like to call themselves "progressive" as a form of self-praise, a state of being, an assertion that their politics represent a higher consciousness than the prejudices of the mob of unthinking deplorables and will lead mankind to a sunny upland where human nature will transcend its baser impulses, and peace and harmony will reign. The hypocrisy of their belief structure will unfold as we learn more about the Progressivism ideology.

Furthermore, Progressivism Isn't progressive—it's recycled and repackaged Marxism for a 21st century audience as you will see throughout this handbook.

Conservatives, independents, and sapient beings should not indulge so-called "Progressives" in this self-deception. We should stop using "Progressive" as a synonym for the noun "Left" or the adjective "left-wing" and use "regressive" or "regressivism" instead. At first, you might be wondering why this antonym is being used—but as we move through this guidebook, chapter by chapter, it will become clearly evident there is no progress for Americans from Progressivism's regressivism—only an Orwellian *1984* future that will fundamentally change America for the worse.

Make no mistake: This neo-Marxist assault has been planned and coordinated for years to strike America where she is weakest: in her innate sense of rightness and fair play. Under so-called Progressive pedagogy, you'll see how quickly we have moved from Dr. Martin Luther King, Jr.'s plea that we judge a man by "the content of his character" and back to "the color of his skin." It's regressivism madness—and if Dr. King could see what is happening to his dream—he would be rolling in his grave.

Who Are the Progressive Left?

Who are the Progressive Left? Answer: They are typically very liberal, highly educated, and majority White—and most say U.S. institutions need to be completely rebuilt because of racial bias per the Pew Research Center.

Although they are one of the smallest political typology groups, Progressive Left are the most politically engaged group in the Democratic coalition. No other group turned out to vote at a higher rate in the 2020 general election, and those who did nearly unanimously voted for Joe Biden. They donated money to campaigns in 2020 at a higher rate than any other Democratic-oriented group.

Politically, the Progressive Left is overwhelmingly Democratic and nearly unanimous in their support for Joe Biden in 2020. Nearly all Progressive Left (98%) either identify with or lean toward the Democratic Party: 46% say they strongly identify with the party. About a third (32%) are independents who lean toward the Democratic Party.

To understand and oppose the post-modernists (i.e., Progressives), the ideas by which they orient themselves must be clearly identified.

First is their new unholy trinity of diversity, equity and inclusion (DEI). Diversity is defined not by opinion, such as viewpoint heterodoxy, but by race, ethnicity or gender identity; equity is no longer the laudable goal of equality of opportunity, but the insistence on equality of outcome; and inclusion is the use of identity-based quotas to attain this misconceived state of equity.

All the classic rights of the West are to be considered secondary to these new values.

Take, for example, freedom of speech—the very pillar of democracy. The Progressives (i.e., post-modernists) refuse to believe that people of good will can exchange ideas and reach consensus.

Their world is instead a Hobbesian nightmare of identity groups warring for power. The Hobbesian Nightmare refers to a chaotic, conflict-torn society in which social strata are immersed in a self-centered perpetual antagonism that culminates in widespread violence in which the state apparatus fails to enforce law and order across its territory.

Second is rejection of the free market—of the very idea that free, voluntary trading benefits everyone. They won't acknowledge that capitalism has lifted up hundreds of millions of people so they can for the first time in history afford food, shelter, clothing, transportation—even entertainment and travel. Those classified as poor in the US (and, increasingly, everywhere else) are able to meet their basic needs. Meanwhile, in once-prosperous Venezuela—until recently the poster-child of the campus radicals—the middle class lines up for toilet paper.

Third, and finally, are the politics of identity. Post-modernists don't believe in individuals. You're an exemplar of your race, sex, or sexual preference. You're also either a victim or an oppressor. No wrong can be done by anyone in the former group, and no good by the latter. Such ideas of victimization do nothing but justify the use of power and engender intergroup conflict.

All these concepts originated with Karl Marx, the 19th-century German philosopher. Marx viewed the world as a gigantic class struggle—the bourgeoisie against the proletariat; the grasping rich against the desperate poor. But wherever his ideas were put into practice—in the Soviet Union, Cuba, Mao's China, Vietnam, and Venezuela, to name just a few—whole economies failed, and tens of millions were killed. We fought a decades-long cold war to stop the spread of those murderous notions. But they're back, in the new guise of identity politics.

The corrupt ideas of the post-modern neo-Marxists (I.e., Progressives) should be consigned to the dustbin of history. Instead, we underwrite their continuance in the very institutions where the central ideas of the West should be transmitted across the generations. Unless we stop, post-modernism will do to America and the entire Western world what it's already done to its universities.

Hate and Fear Are Now Major Motivators on Campus

Almost every university in North America has committed to what is called "social justice," which is the implementation of identity politics through the mechanisms of "diversity, equity, and inclusion." Identity politics divides everyone into one of two categories: evil oppressor or innocent victim.

Through official mandatory policies, universities have transformed academic culture from a quest to discover truth about the world and its beings, to the indoctrination of identity politics and enforcement of "social justice" policies.

In practice, this means the adoption of identity ideology to the exclusion and suppression of other views. An elaborate bureaucracy of "diversity and inclusion" officers are charged with policing thought, speech, and action. Activists, and those who support them, encourage active hate against their alleged oppressors: males, whites, Christians, Asians, Jews, heterosexuals, and cis-normal individuals.

How do we know this? Three ways: First, the vehement rejection of any criticism of or counter-argument to their neo-sexist/racist/bigoted ideological positions, and complete unwillingness to entertain any alternative position to their narratives. Second, the immediate use of the most hateful rhetoric imaginable to designate anyone challenging their position. Third, their immediate and unrestrained demands that the challenger be severely punished and preferably destroyed. Let us take these in order.

In response to any opinion contrary to their own, these activists do not offer counterarguments and contrary evidence. They do not claim that the facts are wrong or the position is untrue. No, they reject the opinion on identity grounds, saying that the challenge denies their existence as people, and that it makes them feel unsafe. Or just that it denies the truth of their sacred narrative, and that the complainant is therefore a heretic, any of whose words must be rejected.

The response on campus to this identity-fueled mob hate and its manifestation in attacks, condemnations, and cancellations is fear. Students fear bad grades if they do not repeat identity politics talking points, and they fear social isolation if they are attacked as enemies of "social justice." Professors fear both students and administrators, especially the "diversity and inclusion" officials whose job it is to weed out dissenters for re-education, punishment, and exile.

Self-censorship by college students is well documented in multiple surveys. A survey by the Foundation for Individual Rights and Expression (FIRE) reported that 83 percent engaged in self-censorship.

How far our colleges and universities have come! From open fellowships of research inquiry and intellectual exchange, they have become seminaries of true believers and doctrine enforcers. Identity politics has divided students, professors, and administrators into warring sexes, races, sexualities, genders, ethnicities, and ablenesses, and mandated hate between them.

Admission and success, once based on academic achievement, merit, and potential, is now based on one's sex, race, sexuality, etc., and one's devotion to the identity politics "social justice" narrative. We have regressed from Enlightenment openness back to a Medieval religious order.

Safeguarding Our Republic From Progressivism Madness

Radical activists now confront America with a host of unsapient policies, subversive activism, and false narratives like the 1619 Project, Black Lives Matter (BLM), and Critical Race Theory (CRT). The Progressives who champion these false and woke critiques threaten who we are as a nation, accompanied by equally radical proposals to remake our basic institutions.

Furthermore, the Progressive activists who lead these woke movements have targeted America's schools to impose a revolutionary transformation on our country and they also seek to transform the family, work, the marketplace, government, law, religion, entertainment, sports—all of American society with neo-Marxist ideologies. This cannot be allowed to happen and now is the time to wake up to this woke Progressivism madness before it's too late to stop it.

America is exceptional not least because of its long traditions of antislavery, abolition, and dedication to civic equality that transcends race. It is one of the least racist countries in the world and its citizens of all races have achieved extraordinary prosperity and liberty. The peoples of the world seek to become American because our nation offers opportunity to all. Woke radical activists must engage in hallucinatory defamation to erase these facts.

Shall We Surrender to Marxist CRT?

The Progressive activists who lead these movements have targeted America's schools as the means by which to impose a revolutionary transformation on our country. These activists believe not only that our schools are the linchpin of our apparatus of racial injustice and oppression but also the means by which to force their so-called "liberation" on America. They will seize our children's minds to seize America's future.

As previously noted, these radical activists seek to transform the family, work, the marketplace, government, law, religion, entertainment, sports— all of American society with neo-Marxist ideologies. Their proposals to accomplish this are sweeping. They include a call to establish "equity" that requires a quasi-totalitarian imposition of job quotas and the suppression of all opposing speech as part of Diversity, Equity, and Inclusion (DEI) programs.

But every such proposal is ultimately a plan to change the way Americans think. They require a transformation of our schools from places that teach students to seek out truth to places that teach students to seek out power so as to revolutionize America. No free people would accept the radicals' plans, so they wish to teach our children to embrace tyranny, by persuading them that tyranny is actually fairness or justice. How does this happen?

- They abuse the authority delegated to the schools to propagandize and coerce a captive audience, who must assent to indoctrination or risk all the damage to career prospects that follows from poor grades.

- They exploit the innocence and naiveté of the impressionable young Americans who are in no position to recognize the falsehoods and distortions embedded in these appeals.

- The proponents of neo-racism—to give this collection of radical critiques a unifying name—most of all wish to impose their theory as a curriculum.

- They intend to compel every person to study that curriculum, from early childhood education through high school, college, graduate study, vocational training, and on-the-job instruction.

Or Shall We Stand and Fight For Our Republic?

We approve wholeheartedly MLK's equality of opportunity—but oppose emphatically neo-racism's forced equity of outcomes (the "equity" portion of DEI) because we uphold the value of human freedom. Freedom is an intellectual as well as a political virtue: the freedom to think for oneself and the freedom of a people to govern themselves are distinguishable but interdependent. Intellectual freedom allows us to pursue the truth, which entails encountering and weighing the validity of conflicting views.

Political freedom is the attempt to frame laws and reach decisions through orderly and peaceful processes that give due weight to the many and often conflicting judgments of the governed. There can be no political freedom without intellectual freedom.

And yet this is exactly what neo-racism demands—the end of intellectual freedom. The proponents of so-called "Antiracism" state this most explicitly when they assert that anyone who dissents from their view that America is a systemically racist nation perpetuates racism and deserves to be silenced.

Neo-racism's proponents explicitly advocate for censorship. Their doctrines brook no disagreement, dissent, skepticism, or demand for evidence. Their position is that the only allowable intellectual position is enthusiastic assent to their dogma.

This sort of intellectual totalitarianism is not new. Neo-racism imitates the logic of Marxism, which uses opposition to its arguments to confirm them. Only a class traitor would doubt the necessity of the revolution. The same self-confirming circularity always accompanies movements that suppress intellectual and political freedom.

Only witches would doubt the prevalence of witches, and therefore the witch-deniers must be condemned as witches. Neo-racism at its core is yet another of the witchcraft hysterias that chronically afflict society. America has never been immune to these disorders. We feel ashamed when we awake from them, but we forget our better selves while we are in the midst of them.

Now is the time to wake up before we do even graver damage—not only to ourselves individually but to our country as a whole. It is a bitter irony of our moment that those who want to drive us into this new hysteria often claim to be "woke." There is no awakening in woke. It is the sleep of reason that produces monsters, and it poses a profound peril to our republic.

3 – Woke, Social Justice, Racist, LGBTQ & Ethnic Studies Programs Are Being Exposed

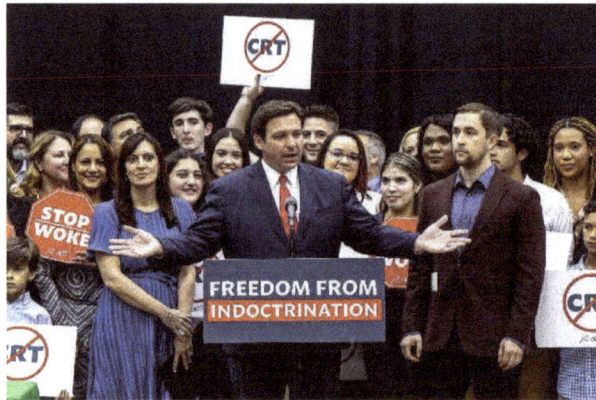

Credit: The Epoch Times–Florida Gov. Ron DeSantis .

Comparing the state of pandemic lockdown statistics, a look at the national map shows that the most populous state, California, is also the most locked down, while the third-most populous, Florida, is almost completely back to normal.

In October 2020, Brown University reported that politics and teachers' union strength best explain how school boards approached reopening. In a September 2020 study, researchers Corey DeAngelis and Christos Makridis found that school districts in places with strong teachers' unions were much less likely to offer full-time, in-person instruction in the fall.

In the early days of the lockdowns, medical experts were mixed on reopening schools, but a solid consensus now exists in favor of doing so. In February 2021, the Center for Disease Control (CDC) urged the nation's elementary and secondary schools to admit students for in-person instruction as soon as possible.

Around the same time, the *New York Times* "asked 175 pediatric disease experts if it was safe enough to open school." The experts, mostly pediatricians focusing on public health, "largely agreed that it was safe enough for schools to be open to elementary students for full-time and in-person instruction now. Some said that this was true even in communities where Covid-19 infections were widespread, as long as basic safety measures were taken." Reopening doesn't lead to increased cases in a community, and closing classrooms "should be a last resort," according to a March 11, 2021, analysis of more than 130 studies by AEI's John Bailey.

The science is also clear that remote learning has been a disaster for children.

A study by FAIR Health, a company that "possesses the nation's largest collection of private healthcare claims data," reveals that young people are suffering profoundly. Comparing August 2019 with August 2020 reveals an almost 334 percent increase in intentional self-harm claims in the Northeast for 13- to 18-year-olds. Drug overdoses more than doubled from April 2019 to April 2020 for the same age cohort. From spring 2020 to November 2020, obsessive-compulsive disorder and tic disorders increased for six- to 12-year-olds.

Additionally, mental-health problems account for a growing proportion of children's visits to hospital emergency rooms. In November, the CDC noted that from March 2020 to October 2020 such visits increased 31 percent for 12- to 17-year-olds and 24 percent for children ages five to 11, compared with the same period in 2019.

Moreover, not all health problems are temporary. Keeping kids away from school will shorten their lifespans, according to the Journal of the American Medical Association.

Beyond the health consequences, school closures also have serious economic ramifications

In September 2020, economists Eric Hanushek and Ludger Woessmann found that accrued lockdown-related learning losses will amount to $14.2 trillion in economic terms.

At last, many liberals in government and the mainstream media joined the conservative chorus calling for an end to school closures.

Veteran *New York Times* columnist Nicholas Kristof, a self-described progressive, is demanding that schools reopen now. In an opinion piece in late February 2021, he blamed "Democratic governors and mayors who too often let schools stay closed even as bars opened." He also stressed that these leaders have "presided over one of the worst blows to the education of disadvantaged Americans in history. The result: more dropouts, less literacy and numeracy, widening race gaps, and long-term harm to some of our most marginalized youth."

Teachers' unions insist that more cash is needed to reopen schools—for masks, updated ventilation systems, and other Covid-related adjustments. But most private schools have been operating safely already without the benefit of budget windfalls.

As policy analyst Inez Stepman writes, only 5 percent of private schools across the country started all-virtual this fall, and they've done it with fewer resources: "Not only is average private school tuition substantially lower than average public school per-pupil funding (about $11,000 vs. public schools' $14,000), they've received only a tiny fraction of the federal and state aid that has been available to public schools."

Money is not the issue; California spends far more per student than Florida, yet Florida was wide open, and California was not.

Parents of all political stripes have reached the end of their rope. Open Schools California and Reopen California Schools have thousands of members statewide. They have called for campuses to reopen, more transparency from school districts, and a seat at the table to discuss reopening plans. Philadelphia-area parents are so frustrated with remote learning that they're running for office, suing, relocating, or retreating to private schools.

Public schools in 33 states have lost 500,000 students in a one-year period, according to an Associated Press-Chalkbeat analysis in December 2020. Data released in February 2021 show that California K-12 public school enrollments have dropped by a record 155,000 students. Nationally, millions have withdrawn from public schools.

It's no surprise that private schools are picking up the slack.

A survey of 160 independent schools found that "121 are currently open full time, for face-to-face learning. The remaining 39 are on some sort of hybrid schedule." Education Week disclosed in November 2020 that the number of homeschooled children nationwide has more than tripled, from 3 percent to 10 percent, and it may be even higher now.

Some parents with financial means have enrolled their children in private schools or formed pandemic pods, but most can't take advantage of these options. The good news: legislatures across the country have begun taking steps to empower parents.

The Educational Freedom Institute reports that 29 states have active legislation devoted to funding students instead of school systems. While red states with weaker teachers' unions are over-represented on the list, blue states are present, too. Massachusetts, Oregon, Minnesota, Maryland, and Washington all have Educational Savings Account legislation in the hopper, and Connecticut lawmakers are considering a tax-credit scholarship proposal.

The teachers' union faithful are attempting to stem the rising tide in favor of school choice. When the pandemic hit in March 2020, the Oregon Education Association successfully lobbied to make it illegal for families to switch to virtual charter schools. Here in California, the heavily union-funded state legislature passed Senate Bill 98 in June 2020. The trailer bill effectively put a moratorium on new charter school enrollments by capping per-student state funding to 2020 funding levels. Had the legislators not done that, charter school enrollments would undoubtedly be surging now.

In a recent survey, Beck Research reported across-the-board support for school-choice policies. Released in January 2021, the Democratic polling outfit found that 65 percent of K-12 parents back school choice. African-Americans (74 percent) and Latinos (71 percent), groups that stand to gain the most from choice, are staunch supporters.

School choice is on the rise today because the teachers' unions, along with their allies in legislatures and educational bureaucracies, have made a mess of things. Finally, however, some states are taking steps in the right direction. It's about time.

How to Combat Gender Theory in Public Schools

As radical gender theory has made its way into public schools across the United States, children as young as five have been exposed to ideas that encourage them to question their gender identities, sometimes with life-changing and irreversible results. Despite Americans' broadly shared skepticism about gender-identity curricula and practices in schools, many ideologically motivated teachers and administrators have not relented in their mission to advance radical gender theory, even in otherwise-conservative areas. Per Christopher F. Rufo:

Among many other examples I've uncovered, in Illinois' Evanston-Skokie School District, kindergarteners read books affirming transgender conversions; in Springfield, Missouri, teacher and administrator training recommends recognizing and affirming a panoply of student gender identities. Over 4,000 schools nationwide feature "gender and sexuality" (GSA) clubs, the national organization which calls for the abolition of the American judicial system and the "cisgender heterosexual patriarchy."

Too often, teachers and administrators keep parents in the dark or pressure them into "affirming" their child's claimed gender identity. Indeed, school policies often advise—or require—teachers not to share gender-related information with parents. Michigan's Department of Education encourages teachers to facilitate students' sexual transitions without parental consent. In Fairfax, Virginia, and Montgomery County, Maryland, teachers are expressly barred from "outing" supposedly transgender children to their parents. The Genders & Sexualities Alliances (GSA) Network instructs adult club "advisors" to keep a child's involvement in a GSA club confidential.

Even where parents learn that their children have adopted a new gender identity, they're often cowed into supporting gender "affirmation" when school officials present them with the Hobson's choice of "a live son or a dead daughter." Worse still, parents who agree to transition their children socially unwittingly invite a form of iatrogenesis— that is, "affirming" their child's newly adopted name, pronouns, and dress in public likely increases the chances of the child's persisting in that identity, which in turn raises the probability of unnecessary medicalization.

These practices are not only deeply misleading; they fly in the face of a century of American law. The Fourteenth Amendment's Due Process Clause protects parents' fundamental right to direct the upbringing, education, and care of their children. States should stand with parents and the Constitution against these intrusions on the family.

Strengthen parents' rights, regulate classroom instruction, and require curriculum transparency.

To that end, I have crafted a policy document designed to guide state legislatures wishing to curb the excesses of radical gender theory in public schools. With the American parents' rights tradition as its lodestar, my proposal seeks to accomplish three main goals.

First, it includes measures to strengthen parents' rights. These include prohibitions on school employees' withholding information from parents about their child's gender identity and health information, engaging in private conversations with students about matters related to sex and gender, or pressuring parents to proceed with "gender affirming" therapies or interventions. School officials would be required to inform parents about any change to their child's health and wellness, and would no longer be allowed, without written parental approval, to affirm a student's gender transition or to address students by names and pronouns other than those indicated on the enrollment forms provided by their parents.

Second, it regulates classroom instruction on sex- and gender-related concepts. As a blanket matter across public schools, it prohibits instruction on human sexuality and gender identity in elementary school, except when required by law as part of the state sex-education curriculum. Parents of children in elementary and middle school would have to provide written consent prior to sex education or instruction on gender-related concepts, and parents of high schoolers would have the ability to opt out of any instruction on such matters. And in response to the disingenuous attacks on Florida's Parental Rights in Education Act, my proposal expressly allows teachers to discuss the presence of same-sex households and human reproduction within a biological context.

Third, building on earlier efforts at the Manhattan Institute to provide transparency in school training and curricula, it requires schools to post on their websites information about sex- and gender-related materials and activities used to instruct students and train teachers and staff. Curriculum transparency is broadly popular, facilitates democratic accountability, and gives parents the information they need to opt in or opt out of classes. My proposal would further require posting information about all school-sponsored clubs, regardless of type, and alert parents of their planned activities.

To be sure, these proposals alone cannot solve the problem of educational institutions captured by gender ideologues and their allies in the teachers' unions. While the law plays a critical role in protecting children and parents, it is not a panacea. Conservatives, moderates, and pragmatists concerned about radical ideologies in their public education institutions must also push back by actively engaging in their children's education, running for school board seats, and even urging their legislators to reinvent public institutions in conformity with the ideals of the American Founding.

Meantime, state law can play an important role in ensuring that parents fulfill their role as recognized under the Constitution. My A Model for School Practices Relating to Sexuality and Gender—Manhattan Institute proposal would go a long way toward achieving that goal. See Appendix for this link.

'Parents' Rights Advocates Running For Local School Board Positions

Across the country, new right-leaning political action committees are pouring money into school board races, aiming to flip control of who governs schools in favor of self-proclaimed parents' rights advocates in a way that rivals the role that teachers unions have historically had in these contests.

For much less than what it would cost them to influence a seat in the House or Senate, these PACs are putting thousands of dollars at a time—sometimes just hundreds—into races for local school boards and as a result, changing education on a national scale.

A super PAC called the 1776 Project PAC is leading the way, emphasizing opposition to lessons related to racial and social justice. With a war chest smaller than what some congressional candidates in competitive districts are raising, the group has supported and opposed school board candidates in a dozen states.

Political action committees, or PACs, and super PACs pool donations from many different people and entities and use that money to try to elect candidates who represent their interests. They may be registered at the federal or state level.

Ian Vandewalker, senior counsel for the democracy program at New York University's Brennan Center for Justice, a left leaning think-tank, said the involvement of these major PACs in local elections is a sign that politics at large have become nationalized and more partisan.

Other PACs are focusing on specific states and races. A grocery store heiress is behind a PAC spending to influence school board races across the state of Florida, and a federal PAC that typically focuses on federal policy got involved in one Florida county. In Texas, a PAC is raising big money to flip school board seats statewide.

Candidates with the most money in their campaign accounts tend to be the ones who win. At the school board level, that effect has the potential to be larger because the races are often so cheap.

Schooled by DeSantis: How to Defeat Union-Backed School Board Candidates

Woody Allen once observed that 80 percent of success in life comes down to showing up.

For decades, conservatives failed to heed this advice in education politics, letting unions monopolize the school boards that govern American K–12 education. That ended on November 8, 2022, as Florida governor Ron

DeSantis helped conservatives defeat a record number of union-backed school board candidates.

Despite conservatives' faith in the virtue of local control, the Right's failure to engineer consistent conservative school board victories has long given Progressives in the education establishment a stranglehold on local school politics.

Decades of research show, for example, that teachers' unions win roughly 70 percent of competitive school board races. What's more, because most school board races are nonpartisan, low-turnout affairs, conservative voters often unwittingly help elect union-friendly board majorities. With no reliable counterweight to hold them accountable, teachers' unions hold outsize power in school board decision-making.

This state of affairs quietly persisted until the pandemic, when conservative (and moderate) parents discovered the price of their apathy and disorganization. Conceding school board seats to the education establishment now had real and visible costs. Union-friendly boards that presided over unjustifiable school closures showed more concern for their politically active employees than they did for the parents and kids struggling with remote schooling.

At the same time, classes on Zoom gave many parents their first-ever look at controversial curricula and instructional materials. Even though a majority of parents oppose elementary students learning about "sex education and LGBTQ issues," establishment forces persisted, with parents reporting one outlandish episode after another during the pandemic-plagued school year. One local union leader in Maine told complaining parents that they should just leave the public schools entirely.

Enter DeSantis

In his victory speech on Election Night, his line, "we fought the woke in the schools [and won]," made all the headlines. But the hard work that enabled this victory came from coordinated electioneering efforts during the quiet summer months leading up to Florida's August primary. DeSantis had put his political muscle behind 30 conservative school board candidates who pledged to support a parents-first and anti-woke agenda.

When the dust settled, DeSantis's conservative school board candidates had prevailed in over 80 percent of their races. More impressive still, in the 19 elections where one of DeSantis's candidates faced a union-backed opponent, the unions won just four races (21 percent). In previous elections in the same districts—when conservatives had no coordinated electioneering effort in place—union-favored candidates won more than 70 percent of their races.

These trends prevailed across the country where conservatives mounted a coordinated electioneering effort as in Florida, they did well. But where conservatives did not make such a push, teachers' unions continued their dominance of school board contests in both red and blue states. My own analysis of union electioneering in red Indiana and blue Michigan, for example, uncovered robust union win rates of 66 and 74 percent, respectively.

In other words, without the coattails of a strong (and coordinated) conservative message in these local races, teachers' unions were able to maintain their historic edge and notch three times as many victories (in percentage terms) in the Midwest as they did in Florida.

There's no reason that the DeSantis/Florida GOP strategy can't work beyond the Sunshine State. Other Republican states had popular governors who stood up to teachers' unions on reopening schools and keeping unwanted and divisive ideology out of the classroom. But showing up matters. Even now, in this time of hotly contested educational controversies, numerous school board seats routinely go uncontested.

In low-salience contests, Progressive school boards can easily endure in conservative communities that don't pay much attention. As Craig DiSesa, who oversees campaign operations for the Virginia-based The Middle Resolution, told me, even in some of the commonwealth's more conservative school districts, liberal boards have persisted because of a lack of political engagement. In 2022, DiSesa's group flipped several school board seats in Virginia Beach, installing school-choice advocates over union-backed establishment figures.

Basic efforts aimed at recruiting better candidates and coordinating small donations from popular conservative officials (DeSantis gave his endorsed candidates $1,000 each) can go a long way toward winning conservative majorities on school boards. The potential return on this investment is huge. Taxpayers and families will benefit by seeing their interests better represented on boards, and conservative lawmakers can begin building a stable of future candidates for other local and state offices.

For conservatives, there's a clear path forward, but they will need to get—and keep—their hands dirty. As the pandemic subsides and normalcy returns to our schools, conservatives cannot afford to take their eyes off these crucial down-ballot races.

With an Anti-Wokeness Platform

4 – America's Critical Race Theory Battles: Florida vs. California

Credit: Education Next.

Critical race theory is fast becoming America's new institutional orthodoxy. Yet most Americans have never heard of it—and of those who have, many don't understand it. This must change. We need to know what it is so we can know how to fight it.

To explain critical race theory, it helps to begin with a brief history of Marxism. Originally, the Marxist Left built its political program on the theory of class conflict. Karl Marx believed that the primary characteristic of industrial societies was the imbalance of power between capitalists and workers. The solution to that imbalance, according to Marx, was revolution: the workers would eventually gain consciousness of their plight, seize the means of production, overthrow the capitalist class, and usher in a new socialist society.

However, during the twentieth century, a number of regimes underwent Marxist-style revolutions, and each ended in disaster. Socialist governments in the Soviet Union, China, Cambodia, Cuba, and elsewhere racked up a body count of nearly 100 million people. They are remembered for gulags, show trials, executions, and mass starvations. In practice, Marx's ideas unleashed man's darkest brutalities.

By the mid-1960s, Marxist intellectuals in the West had begun to acknowledge these failures. They recoiled at revelations of Soviet atrocities and came to realize that workers' revolutions would never occur in Western Europe or the United States, which had large middle classes and rapidly improving standards of living. Americans in particular had never developed a sense of class consciousness or class division. Most Americans believed in the American dream—the idea that they could transcend their origins through education, hard work, and good citizenship.

But rather than abandon their political project, Marxist scholars in the West simply adapted their revolutionary theory to the social and racial unrest of the 1960s. Abandoning Marx's economic dialectic of capitalists and workers, they substituted race for class and sought to create a revolutionary coalition of the dispossessed based on racial and ethnic categories.

Fortunately, the early proponents of this revolutionary coalition in the U.S. lost out in the 1960s to the civil rights movement, which sought instead the fulfillment of the American promise of freedom and equality under the law. Americans preferred the idea of improving their country to that of overthrowing it. Martin Luther King Jr.'s vision, President Lyndon Johnson's pursuit of the Great Society, and the restoration of law and order promised by President Richard Nixon in his 1968 campaign defined the post-1960s American political consensus.

But the radical Left has proved resilient and enduring—which is where critical race theory comes in.

Critical race theory is an academic discipline, formulated in the 1990s and built on the intellectual framework of identity-based Marxism. Relegated for many years to universities and obscure academic journals, it has increasingly become the default ideology in our public institutions over the past decade. It has been injected into government agencies, public school systems, teacher training programs, and corporate human-resources departments, in the form of diversity-training programs, human-resources modules, public-policy frameworks, and school curricula.

Its supporters deploy a series of euphemisms to describe critical race theory, including "equity," "social justice," "diversity and inclusion," and "culturally responsive teaching." Critical race theorists, masters of language construction, realize that "neo-Marxism" would be a hard sell.

Equity, on the other hand, sounds non-threatening and is easily confused with the American principle of equality.

But the distinction is vast and important. Indeed, critical race theorists explicitly reject equality—the principle proclaimed in the Declaration of Independence, defended in the Civil War, and codified into law with the Fourteenth and Fifteenth Amendments, the Civil Rights Act of 1964, and the Voting Rights Act of 1965. To them, equality represents "mere nondiscrimination" and provides "camouflage" for white supremacy, patriarchy, and oppression.

In contrast to equality, equity as defined and promoted by critical race theorists is little more than reformulated Marxism. In the name of equity, UCLA law professor and critical race theorist Cheryl Harris has proposed suspending private property rights, seizing land and wealth, and redistributing them along racial lines. Critical race guru Ibram X. Kendi, who directs the Center for Antiracist Research at Boston University, has proposed the creation of a federal Department of Antiracism. This department would be independent of (i.e., unaccountable to) the elected branches of government, and would have the power to nullify, veto, or abolish any law at any level of government and curtail the speech of political leaders and others deemed insufficiently "antiracist."

One practical result of the creation of such a department would be the overthrow of capitalism, since, according to Kendi, "In order to truly be antiracist, you also have to truly be anti-capitalist." In other words, identity is the means; Marxism is the end.

An equity-based form of government would mean the end not only of private property but also of individual rights, equality under the law, federalism, and freedom of speech. These would be replaced by race-based redistribution of wealth, group-based rights, active discrimination, and omnipotent bureaucratic authority. Historically, the accusation of "anti-Americanism" has been overused. But in this case, it's not a matter of interpretation: critical race theory prescribes a revolutionary program that would overturn the principles of the Declaration and destroy the remaining structure of the Constitution.

Florida v. Critical Race Theory

Over the past two years, Florida Governor DeSantis has emerged as one of the most articulate political spokesmen for the anti–critical race theory movement. His new policy agenda builds on successful anti-CRT legislation in other states but goes two steps further.

First, it provides parents with a "private right of action," which allows them to sue offending institutions for violations, gain information through legal discovery, and, if they win in the courts, collect attorney's fees.

Second, it tackles critical race theory in corporate "diversity, equity, and inclusion" training programs, which, DeSantis says, sometimes promote racial stereotyping, scapegoating, and harassment, in violation of state civil rights laws.

Following one of his speeches, DeSantis invited Christopher F. Rufo, America's leading anti-woke spokesperson and journalist, to address the crowd. Rufo explained that the reason critical race theory has upset so many Americans is that it speaks to two deep reservoirs of human sentiment: citizens' desire for self-government and parents' desire to shape the moral and educational development of their children. Elite institutions have attempted to step between parent and child.

DeSantis has deftly positioned himself as a protector of middle-American families. One of the guest speakers, Lacaysha Howell, a biracial mother from Sarasota, said that left-wing teachers tried to persuade her daughter that the white side of their family was oppressive.

Another speaker, Eulalia Jimenez, a Cuban-American mother from the Miami area, said that left-wing indoctrination in schools reminded her of her father's warnings about Communism in his native Cuba. Both believed that critical race theory was poison to the American Dream.

Furthermore, Florida legislators have the opportunity to craft the gold standard for "culture war" policy. The governor's team has worked with a range of interested parties, including the Manhattan Institute, which has crafted model language for prohibiting racialist indoctrination and providing curriculum transparency to parents.

The battle is ultimately about shaping public policy in accord with public values. "I think we have an ability [to] just draw a line in the sand and say, 'That's not the type of society that we want here in the state of Florida,'" said DeSantis. The stakes are high—and all eyes are on Florida to deliver.

No Cause for Controversy

When Florida governor Ron DeSantis signed the "Parental Rights in Education" bill into law, banning public school teachers from kindergarten through third grade from holding classroom instruction on sexual orientation and gender identity, most Progressives saw it as an attack on LGBT rights.

Overnight, the inflammatory and misleading moniker "Don't Say Gay" was applied to the new law, setting off alarms across the country. Hysteria over Florida's mischaracterized "Don't Say Gay" law largely involves obscuring the fact that it applies only to children under age ten.

New York City mayor Eric Adams launched a digital campaign in five Florida markets to condemn the law, while the ACLU began its own campaign: "Just Say 'No' to 'Don't Say Gay.'" The ACLU suggested that the Florida law could keep classic authors like Langston Hughes and American poet Walt Whitman out of school libraries. Former presidential candidate Pete Buttigieg said that the law would result in suicides of young LGBT people.

NPR's coverage of the story skirted objectivity when it highlighted the view that the law would hurt LGBT children, despite DeSantis's claim that the law would merely safeguard toddlers from a "woke gender ideology." Progressives are also fixating on what Florida state representative Joe Harding, the House bill's sponsor, was quoted as saying: that classroom instruction on such topics could be prohibited beyond third grade if it was determined not to be "age or developmentally appropriate."

There's much to unpack here, namely: Are first- and second-graders liable to commit suicide because their local public school will not support their emerging gender identity? On the contrary, the notion that third-graders

41

can be aware of themselves as "trans" is a fantasy produced by the woke narrative industry.

There likely isn't a third-grader in the world who would find it necessary to jump from a tall building because his trans identity (and where would he have gotten this notion, anyway, at such a tender age?) is not taken seriously at school. What Buttigieg and others are really arguing for is preparatory training for schoolchildren on these issues, so that, if the kids eventually come out as LGB (but more likely trans), they will have already been "primed" in these matters.

The *Wall Street Journal* correctly observed that reaction to the bill in many quarters, both for and against, is overwrought. The bill's opponents aren't part of a covert operation literally to seduce young school children into sex. The "grooming" at issue here would be better termed "woke gender indoctrination." Meantime, the White House has joined the hysteria on the other side, referring to the bill as "cruel."

As then White House press secretary Jen Psaki said, "It is certainly something that is not helping, you know, young people who are members of the LGBTQI+ community who are already vulnerable, already being bullied."

There appears to be universal consensus on the part of Progressives to ignore the fact that the law refers only to young children slightly past toddler age and not "youth" maturing into sexual awareness.

Critical Race Theory: Its Origins and Infiltration of California Public Schools

In California, the teaching of critical race theory in K-12 schools has become widespread as school districts, virtually en masse, have adopted DEI and ethnic studies curricula laden with CRT. The California State Board of Education—an eleven-member board that oversees the California Department of Education—adopted a 700-page Ethnic Studies Model Curriculum in 2021. This model curriculum adheres to a liberated ethnic studies philosophy.

The curriculum's list of guiding values includes "challenging racist, bigoted, discriminatory, and imperialist/colonial beliefs and practices on multiple levels" and the "struggle for social justice...transformative resistance, critical hope, and radical healing."

Also in 2021, the state passed AB 101, which adds ethnic studies coursework to the list of requirements for high school graduation. Izumi, Wu, and Richards, authors of *The Great Parent Revolt: How Parents and Grassroots Leaders Are Fighting Critical Race Theory in America's Schools,* note that at least 20 California school districts quickly endorsed liberated ethnic studies model curriculum even before the bill was passed. Under AB 101, districts are not mandated to use the state's Model Curriculum, but are required to offer an ethnic studies course by 2025.

CRT proponents quickly moved to capitalize on the state's mandate by securing lucrative contracts with school districts to implement liberated ethnic studies curricula. California schools and districts are purchasing these curricula at great expense to taxpayers.

For example, Salinas Union High School hired a Liberated Ethnic Studies Model Curriculum consultant at $1,500 per hour.

In 2022, Castro Valley Unified School District's board unanimously approved an $82,560 contract with the Liberated Ethnic Studies Model Curriculum Coalition—despite the objections of community members who expressed their disapproval of the contract due to the coalition's anti-Semitic leanings. Hayward Unified also approved a contract with the same group in 2022, which is reported to have cost the district $35,395 (while other reports say Hayward will need to spend $40 million on "recruiting, training, and materials").

In 2020, Jefferson Elementary School District in San Mateo County approved a $40,000 contract for Ethnic Studies curriculum for "3-4 schools," which amounts to $10,000 or more per school. The contract includes a "consultant keynote" costing $8,500.

San Diego Unified's 2022-23 LCAP (Local Control Accountability Plan, a report published each year that describes a district's goals and expenditures) admits huge sums of taxpayer dollars for CRT-inspired actions. Pages 36-38 list three actions, costing a combined $3,243,854, to "implement Anti-Bias, Anti-Racism pedagogy and practices" with "Site Equity Teams" and the disruption of so-called "discriminatory grading practices." Page 103 of the plan reports $1,261,602 for "anti-bias, anti-racism training," further development of the Site Equity Teams, and "Affinity Groups" and professional networks for employees to discuss their lived experiences concerning race.

How are we seeing CRT implemented in California?

The Great Parent Revolt sheds light on several concerning examples that illustrate the havoc CRT is causing in the state:

In 2021, news broke that third grade students at R.I. Meyerholz Elementary School in Cupertino were told to create "identity maps" in math class (yes, math). An identity map lists a person's traits such as race, causing the person to consider the degree to which they are an oppressor or victim.

In 2020 in Orange County, a seven-year old girl wrote "All Life" on a Black Lives Matter drawing that she had made. The school deemed the girl's action to be unacceptable and forced her to apologize. You read that correctly: the school made the seven-year old student apologize for expressing that all life matters. Her mother, who sued the district, says that her daughter was required to sit out at recess and publicly apologize on the playground.

San Francisco Unified cut advanced math classes for the sake of "racial equity," forcing all students in each respective grade to take the same math courses. This meant that students ready for advanced classes were relegated to less challenging courses that were ill-suited for them. A group of 50 concerned parents and grandparents in the district filed a lawsuit against the district in 2023, saying that students are adversely impacted by the district's move.

In 2021, a gay white father of a biracial student was turned down from joining a San Francisco Unified volunteer parent committee because he didn't contribute to the racial "diversity" of the board. This highlights CRT's practical out workings: an individual's qualifications are judged based on race, and diversity is defined in terms of ethnicity or skin color, which overrides other types of diversity.

Teachers unions are a driving force behind the adoption of Critical Race Theory throughout California schools. A traditional view of race and ethnic studies seeks a society where—in the spirit of Dr. Martin Luther King Jr.'s vision—all people are judged based on their character and known by their unique personalities and strengths, since race is a non-essential aspect of what makes a person unique.

In contrast, the California Teachers Association (CTA) says it aims to "amplify the intersections of race, gender, language, sexual orientation, class, ableism, etc." This amplification emphasizes our differences, rather than what unites us as a society.

This gets to the heart of the problem with CRT: the hyper-focus on oppression is antithetical to the spirit of American unity. Constructive ethnic studies promotes education about historical oppression, while maintaining that real reforms have been made and that people of all races in America can work together to make positive contributions to society.

In sharp contrast, liberated ethnic studies maintains that America, and the West at large, is systematically, inherently, and irredeemably racist toward nonwhites. Yet, scores of immigrants of all races, fleeing corruption, poverty, and oppression, have come to the US to take part in the American Dream. The conception of America put forward by liberated ethnic studies and CRT seems to forget that reality.

Yet the California Federation of Teachers (CFT) and California Teachers Association (CTA) stand in opposition to these ideals. Both unions spend hundreds of millions of dollars each election cycle on supporting political candidates—from local school board trustees to state and federal representatives—who write and enact policies requiring ethnic studies curriculum in schools.

Follow The Money data reveals that the author and 34 bill sponsors of AB 101 (a total of 35 Assemblymembers) received political contributions from the California Teachers Association, California Federation of Teachers, or both—every single one. In fact, both unions are among the Top 10 contributors for 27 out of these 35 politicians, and among the Top 20 contributors for 33 of them.

Resisting Critical Race Theory

But some school districts and county boards of education are resisting the CRT tsunami. In July and August of 2021, the Orange County Board of Education held two educational forums, involving expert testimony and public comment, to expose what CRT really is, its connection to liberated ethnic studies, and the effects of its implementation in schools. Izumi, Wu, and Richards write that these "were the first such events sponsored by an elected educational body in the country."

In August 2021, the Paso Robles Joint Unified School District board voted to ban CRT's teachings from its classrooms. The resolution lists thirteen specific elements and doctrines of CRT that "cannot be taught" in the district's schools, including: that "only individuals classified as 'white' people can be racist because only 'white' people control society," that "an individual, by virtue of his or her race or sex, is inherently racist and/or sexist, whether consciously or unconsciously," and that "individuals are either a member of the oppressor class or the oppressed class because of race or sex."

Temecula Valley School District's board passed a very similar resolution banning the same CRT elements and doctrines in December 2022. It notes that "Critical Race Theory assigns generational guilt and racial guilt for conduct and policies that are long in the past." The resolution also states that the board "desires to uplift and unite students by not imposing the responsibility of historical transgressions in the past and will instead engage students of all cultures in age-appropriate critical thinking."

Critical race theory is still being infused into schools throughout California and across America, but school board trustees and parents aren't letting it go unchallenged. Parents, grandparents, and concerned citizens can take action in the following ways:

Find out what curriculum is being taught in your neighborhood's schools by filing a Public Records Act (PRA) request. Public schools are government-run, government-funded entities. Therefore, they are legally obligated to comply with records requests, and this extends to the curriculum they implement.

See the California Policy Center (CPC) Parent Union's guide to filing a PRA request for help getting started, and their other guides below in the Appendix.

Monitor your children's assignments and textbooks they bring home. Some buzzwords in the curricula that point to liberated ethnic studies and CRT are restorative justice; social justice; white privilege; radical healing; intersectionality; implicit bias; and dominant narratives.

Wenyuan Wu at the Californians for Equal Rights Foundation has published a helpful resource for identifying CRT. Common denominators of CRT instruction are that: 1) Race is front and center, 2) Most observed adverse outcomes in our society are attributed to institutional or systemic racism, and 3) Students and participants are often called to engage in political calls for action and activism.

If you want to engage with your school district about what's being taught in your community's classrooms, check out CPC Parent Union's resource on how to hold your school board accountable.

It's also crucial to remain aware of legislation coming out of Sacramento that affects schools throughout the state. To learn about how to be an effective advocate during the legislative session, don't miss this in-depth guide on how to influence the legislative process.

Concerned citizens can also connect with advocacy groups like the Alliance for Constructive Ethnic Studies (ACES), which has spearheaded efforts to educate voters and school board trustees, and lobbies the legislature concerning ethnic studies legislation. The Californians for Equal Rights Foundation is another California-based group pushing back against CRT.

The Great Parent Revolt authors Izumi, Wu, and Richards note that from 2014-2019, voter turnout for school board elections in America ranged from 5 to 10 percent. While turnout seems to have increased slightly since 2019, it is still critical for concerned parents to show up at the ballot box. School board members make decisions about the curricula used in your schools, and you get a say in who sits on the school boards because they're elected positions.

When expressing your concern or frustration about CRT at school board meetings or with teachers, school administrators, and fellow parents, remember that you aren't alone. While CRT claims to be the enlightened, tolerant position, you know enough about it to see through its deception. By being aware of CRT's tenets and doctrines, you will be equipped to identify its harmful messages, and you can prepare your children to do the same.

5 – The Need for Curriculum Transparency is Clear

Credit: National Review.

Under Governor DeSantis, Florida has taken the lead in advancing online curriculum transparency and likewise, Florida's teachers unions have just gone 0 for 2 in their recent bid to stop Florida's groundbreaking education reforms.

While Vice President Kamala Harris and teachers union boss Randi Weingarten unsuccessfully sought to smear the state's new social studies standards in July 2023, the unions suffered an even bigger curricular defeat later that summer over the state's new online curriculum transparency law.

Earlier in 2023, the state's teachers union—the Florida Education Association (FEA)—filed to block the implementation of Florida's 2022 online curriculum transparency legislation, which requires each public school district to "publish on its website, in a searchable format prescribed by the department, a list of all instructional materials" and a "list of all materials maintained in the school library media center or required as part of a school or grade-level reading list."

Taking a page from its usual playbook, the union attempted to argue that implementation of the curriculum transparency legislation would be prohibitively costly. But as the administrative law judge hearing the case concluded this past month, the union's talking points amounted to little more than hot air and hysteria. For instance, as the court noted:

"Ms. Pat Barber, president of MEA [teachers union], testified about the purported effects of the rules on teachers and media specialists... citing as a 'cost,' the decision by the Manatee County School District to offer non-contracted hourly pay to media specialists for them to complete work outside their normal work schedules."

But as the judge pointed out, this façade was little more than a smokescreen that not even the union representative herself believed:

"In fact, in her deposition taken six days prior to the final hearing, Ms. Barber was unaware of any media specialists who had been paid non contracted hours in order to comply with the Rules. Ms. Barber's testimony at the final hearing, in which she claimed to be aware of non-contracted hourly work, is not credible, is rejected as unpersuasive, and was based largely on hearsay."

More broadly, the court recognized that school districts were already equipped to implement the online curriculum transparency legislation with minimal cost:

"Most districts already had a computerized system in place for cataloging materials (i.e. 'Destiny'); districts were not required to purchase any new system or software (the districts could post the information in a 'PDF' document format); and the cataloging requirement was flexible."

In short, the only real barrier stopping public schools from disclosing online what they are presenting to students is... union opposition. Indeed, as the state's commissioner of education, Manny Diaz Jr., summarized, "It's sad to see the Florida teachers' union waste their members' hard-earned money on a frivolous lawsuit to block parents from knowing what their children are reading in classrooms."

Under the legislation signed by Gov. Ron DeSantis, Florida has taken the lead in advancing online curriculum transparency. Now, it is up to the

Sunshine State or others to build on this foundation and enact the provisions of the full Academic Transparency Act to ensure that all supplemental material—whether essays like the 1619 Project or other politically activist articles or videos—presented to students are disclosed to parents and the public online.

Next Step for the Parents' Movement: Curriculum Transparency

In 2021, public school parents vaulted to the forefront of America's fractured political landscape. Around the country, parents objected both to Covid-related school closures and to racially divisive curricula. Parental frustration helped secure sweeping GOP wins in Virginia, highlighted by Glenn Youngkin's victory over former governor Terry McAuliffe. Youngkin has promised to rein in public-school radicalism and "ban critical race theory" on his first day in office.

Perhaps the central moment in the Virginia gubernatorial race was McAuliffe's comment during a debate: "I don't think parents should be telling schools what they should teach." Like most Virginia voters, they couldn't disagree more. Research shows that greater academic success follows when parents actively engage in their children's education.

To be sure, this doesn't mean that they should decide the finer points of curricular design by plebiscite; nor does it mean that a minority of objecting parents should dictate school pedagogy. But public schools are institutions created by "We the People" and should be responsive to the input of parents and the broader voting public at the state and local level.

At a minimum, parents should be able to know what's being taught to their children in the classroom. Transparency is a virtue for all of our public institutions, but especially for those with power over children.

To that end, a new policy document produced by the Manhattan Institute provides model language designed to promote transparency in public-school curricula. Compiled by experts James R. Copland, Christopher F. Rufo, and John Ketcham, the document recognizes that the finer points of curricular design need not be directed by plebiscite, but that states can provide parents with a pathway for reviewing materials and objecting to those that a plurality would consider flagrantly misguided.

The team's "A Model for Transparency in School Training and Curriculum" model language can be found in the Appendix.

The time since 2020 has demonstrated the need for transparency measures. As many public schools migrated to "virtual only" learning in response to the pandemic, parents received a first-hand look at the divisive, racialist curricula being taught to their children.

They learned that public schools were forcing third-graders to deconstruct their racial and sexual identities, showing kindergarteners dramatizations of dead black children and warning them about "racist police," and telling white teachers that they were guilty of "spirit murdering" minorities. These were not isolated incidents.

These revelations prompted parents to demand to know exactly what was being taught to their children. They felt that the public-school bureaucracies had been hiding controversial materials and exerting undue influence over their children, all in the service of fashionable left-wing ideologies.

Frustrated parents understandably pushed back.

Frustrated parents understandably pushed back, protested at school board meetings, and, in some cases, forced the resignations of school superintendents who refused to listen to their concerns. School officials often responded to parents' concerns with resentment. Some were so agitated by the parental pushback that they sought federal intervention—including through a well-publicized (and since retracted) letter from the National School Boards Association (NSBA) comparing parents to "domestic terrorists."

Other school officials insisted that they, not parents and not voters, should be in charge of children's pedagogy. This is precisely backward. While government schools necessarily cannot meet every parent's demands, parents have a fundamental right, long recognized in law, to guide their children's education and moral conscience. To exercise those rights, parents need accurate information about the learning materials and activities their kids are encountering in government schools.

It does not attempt to define specific concepts, methods, or ideologies. Nor does it seek to ban, restrict, or discourage any materials, activities, or pedagogies. Its aim is simply to provide parents with information about the curricula used in the classroom across all subjects—and to let families, teachers, and schools negotiate disagreements at the local level. If they cannot resolve their differences, parents have options: petition elected leaders or run for school board seats themselves, move to a different area, or remove their children from the public school system.

By focusing on transparency, our prescriptions sidestep arguments about "censorship" in public schools. Realistically speaking, any school necessarily has to pick and choose what to teach among near-infinite options.

Openness will not necessarily engender trust. Parents will certainly disagree about pedagogy. There's no simple way to reconcile all competing perspectives. But the answer to these inevitable disagreements cannot be to hide from parents what's being taught to their own children. They believe that funding common schools in our democratic system requires information and engagement—and so they propose that public schools open their books and let parents see what's inside.

The Fight for Curriculum Transparency

The debate over America's public schools, which began in 2020 with Covid-19-related closures and continued in 2021 with the backlash against critical race theory, has shifted to a third phase: curriculum transparency where parents have the right to know what public schools are teaching their children. Per Christopher F. Rufo:

Last December 2021, my Manhattan Institute colleagues Jim Copland, John Ketcham, and I developed a model transparency policy, which, if adopted, would require public schools to make teaching materials available to parents online. Since then, legislators in 19 states have introduced bills to require curriculum transparency statewide. It has become, within a matter of weeks, one of the hottest public-policy ideas in the country—and, just as quickly, one of the most controversial.

As soon as conservative legislators began introducing these bills, left-wing activist organizations lined up in opposition. In states such as Kansas and Indiana, teachers' unions have rallied their members to state capitols to protest curriculum transparency. The unions object to any imposition on teachers, but they also fear—after the unprecedented public anger generated by school closures, mask mandates, and critical race theory—that giving parents a window into the classroom will strengthen the backlash.

They should be worried. In recent years, teachers' unions have been captured by their most radical elements. The National Education Association (NEA), which represents more than 3 million public school employees, explicitly endorsed critical race theory and other radical ideologies. The organization is fighting to block parents from knowing whether its members have implemented these unpopular pedagogies in the classroom.

Civil rights organizations have also moved to block greater transparency in public schools. The American Civil Liberties Union (ACLU), which once vigorously supported legislation to provide government transparency, recently abandoned this principle. "Some of these so-called 'curriculum transparency bills' are thinly veiled attempts at chilling teachers and students from learning and talking about race and gender in schools," said ACLU staff attorney Emerson Sykes. "We are actively pursuing litigation to block these laws and policies."

Even more absurdly, one activist associated with the "free speech" organization PEN America told NPR that "school transparency is essentially this Big Brother-type regime" that could be used to "intimidate and punish instructors." This inversion would make Orwell blush: in 1984, Big Brother was the government monitoring the people; now, to some left-wing activists, Big Brother is the people monitoring the government. For the ACLU and PEN America, speech is violence, transparency is censorship, and democracy is tyranny.

Conservative legislators should not be deterred. The case for curriculum transparency rests on an irrefutable moral argument: parents have the right to know what the government is teaching their children. Parents are not only taxpayers but also the primary stakeholders in the public education system. Approximately 90 percent of American families entrust their children's education to public schools.

That system's minimum responsibility is to provide accurate, timely, and comprehensive information about the curriculum—especially as it relates to sensitive and controversial topics such as race, gender, identity, and political ideology. The recent parent backlash underscores the importance of transparency. Millions of American families feel that the public schools are working against their values. Transparency legislation is the bare minimum for public schools to start rebuilding trust with these families.

Curriculum transparency has been a political winner, too. As I explained in January 2022, after the victory of anti-critical race theory legislation in 2021, the Left hoped that conservatives would overplay their hand. No such luck: by supporting curriculum transparency, conservatives have baited the Left into opposing a non-threatening, liberal value once embraced by citizens of all political stripes.

To prove this point, organizations like the ACLU immediately abandoned their principles to protect the interests of teachers' unions and entrenched powers. "The ACLU of old would never have argued for government secrecy, especially when it comes to public schools," Zaid Jilani wrote. "America still needs the commitment to government transparency that the ACLU once exemplified. One might even say that we need it more than ever."

The race is now on to see which governor will become the first in the nation to sign curriculum transparency into law. He or she will not only honor parents' right to know what their children are being taught in the classroom but also initiate the long and necessary process of rebalancing the relationship between public schools and the public.

The ultimate goal of curriculum-transparency legislation is to restore trust in the school system and provide families with a mechanism for accountability. Good teachers will have no problem sharing their lessons and working with parents; bad or ideologically motivated teachers, on the other hand, will be exposed to parental oversight and can be held responsible by administrators. That is how good government is supposed to work.

School Transparency Wars

As states and school boards battle over school curricula, the least we can do is keep parents informed about what their kids are learning.

Bologna. The FDA insists that every last ingredient of the heavily processed food is listed on the package label. No one has an issue with that because it's important to know what we put into our bodies. You might think the same mentality would be in place for what goes into our minds, especially those of children, but unfortunately that has become a very contentious issue.

With the revelation that too many of government-run k-12 schools have turned into indoctrination mills, there is now pushback from parents. As reported by Christopher Rufo, lawmakers in 19 states have introduced bills that require curriculum transparency.

So, who could possibly be against transparency? First and foremost, the teachers unions. In 2021, a mother was sued by the Rhode Island state affiliate of the National Education Association (NEA) after she made a public records request to find out exactly what her daughter was going to be taught in kindergarten.

In the Hoosier State, the Indiana State Teachers Association is currently battling against House Bill 1134, which would require teachers to post school curricula online. In Utah, the state teachers union is trying to fend off HB 234, a bill that would require educators to disclose what they are teaching. Unions in other states are fighting similar battles.

Additionally, a teacher union official recently wrote a sarcastic post on Facebook, mocking parents' calls for transparency, suggesting that they butt out of school affairs. Owen Jackman, a California Teachers Association state council delegate and teacher in the Sacramento City Unified School District, equated parents who advocate for their kids at school board meetings to "storm troopers."

Jackman joked that he has "a reason to be concerned about the appropriateness of what your child is learning outside of school." He went on to request that parents "provide a play-by-play of the television shows their kids watch, the social media they use, swear words and racial epithets their kids hear each day, the books being read to them, and activities they will participate in for the remainder of the year." Jackman seems to think he shares parenting responsibilities with mom and dad.

New York Magazine writer Sarah Jones is certainly on the anti-transparency bandwagon. In a recent piece, she referred to parents as "household tyrants," and insists that the call for parental transparency is a wacko Christian Republican plot. She states that since schools don't interfere with a child's life at home, parents should butt out at school.

At the same time, NBC News alerts us that "conservative activists want schools to post lesson plans online, but free speech advocates warn such policies could lead to more censorship in K-12 schools." NBC national reporter Tyler Kingkade adds, "Some of the proposals under consideration in state legislatures, including a bill in Missouri, would require schools to post all teacher training materials online, in addition to descriptions of what is taught." The bill has drawn criticism from Democrats, including state Rep. Maggie Nurrenbern, who called the proposal "an attempt to undermine public education."

Undermine public education? Hardly. Parents who send their children to public schools are not trying to undermine them. In reality, they are seriously concerned about the political indoctrination and sexual grooming that too many schools are partaking in. Also, the ongoing conflation of transparency and censorship is a redder-than-red herring.

Despite the fearmongering from teacher unionistas, the mainstream media and groups purporting to be in favor of civil rights, our government-run schools are practically begging to be scrutinized. For example:

Washington state teachers are told to hide student gender transitions from parents. These guidelines apply to all K-12 public schools, so it includes children as young as five years old.

The parents of a Florida teenager have filed a federal civil rights lawsuit after their daughter's middle school directed their child to pursue a gender transition without notifying them.

A teacher at the Santa Barbara Unified School District in California, has revealed that teachers have access to a password-protected portal for teaching "culturally responsive material." She notes that the content is far-left, and that parents and the community cannot access the curriculum.

Also in California, a black and now ex-teacher in Salinas reports that while "public education officials are doing their best to convince concerned parents that an ideology that falsely insists America was founded on systemic racism and that our institutions still discriminate against black Americans like me is not being taught to children"—they are lying. She explains, "Children were learning about the so-called four I's of oppression (institutional, internalized, ideological, and interpersonal). The course syllabus said students would use colored strings to 'rank' their different identities to create 'intersectional rainbows.' And the class even included a 'privilege quiz' instructing students to determine how marginalized—or privileged—they were."

As battles in various statehouses rage on over what kids should be taught in school, whatever is decided, parents have a right to know. And since taxpayers fork over billions of dollars every year to the government education complex, they, too, need to be in the loop.

Transparency is paramount. You wouldn't think this would be a contentious issue. The government makes sure we are aware of every ingredient that goes into the bologna we buy. Similarly, we should also know the contents of the curricular bologna kids are being fed in school.

6 – American Parents Revolt

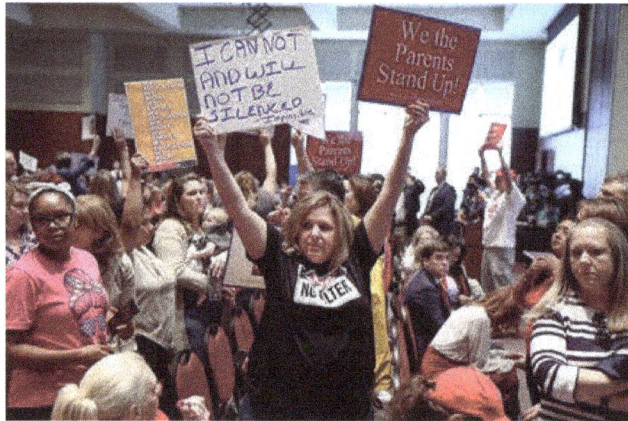

Credit: REUTERS/Evelyn Hockstein–Shelley Slebrch and other angry
parents at Loudoun County School Board meeting.

A great way to stay apprised of issues affecting your school district is to attend school board meetings. It's also your opportunity to make your voice heard when the board takes public comments. Establish a good rapport with your school board by getting to know the members, and know who represents your trustee area on the board.

If you have a concern you'd like to be addressed, prepare a brief statement ahead of time—it's always best to come prepared! A great tool is to look up your board's agenda for the next meeting; be aware that some boards only allow public comment on the agenda items listed for the particular meeting at hand.

One way to ensure your district school board or county Board of Education takes your comments seriously is to attend meetings as a group with other parents. When greater numbers of parents show up to comment on a particular issue, boards take notice.

Attending meetings as a group is also a great way to streamline public comment opportunities because, if you wish, you can choose a "representative" to give a statement, and speakers who follow the speaker can simply state that they agree. Another effective strategy is to put your concerns in writing, and to provide your written letter to the board members and/or their staff.

California's Parent Union David vs. Goliath Battle

In teacher's union dominated California, the Parent Union is a coalition of parents, parent groups, education reform advocates and community leaders dedicated to advancing meaningful education policies, accountability and choice in California's K-12 education system.

For the last several decades, California's public school system has been controlled by the state's powerful teachers union lobby. The result is a school system where 8 out of 10 students can't meet grade level math standards and more than half of students don't read at grade-level. Teachers unions spend hundreds of millions of dollars in teacher member dues each year for lobbying and political spending to oppose every effort to hold schools—and teachers unions—accountable for failing California's kids.

Today, parents throughout California have said "enough is enough." Parents are standing up for students and families at school board meetings, demanding action by state legislators, and running for their local school board to right what is wrong with California's schools.

Parent Union provides training and resources to our members, and brings parents and education reform advocates together to learn, lead and win in the battle to transform California's education system so that every child receives the high-quality education they deserve.

The Parent Union partners with parent groups throughout California and their shared mission is to put students and parents first, improve California's public schools and increase transparency and accountability in our education system.

The Parent Union's Parental Rights Pledge states that we recognize that when a child is born, the family is the primary and responsible governing body for that child. The United States Supreme Court has repeatedly declared and confirmed that parents have the fundamental liberty and pre-political rights to direct the upbringing, care and education of their children as they see fit. The government cannot abridge, suppress, restrict or remove parental rights without due process of law. The same rights apply to legal guardians.

In the exact words of the Parental Rights Pledge:

- I agree that parental rights encompass the freedom to choose any educational opportunity for their children which may include public, private, religious, or home schools, or any other suitable educational options. Parents and guardians should be involved in every aspect of their child's education at all grade levels.

- I agree that school teachers and administrators should be open, honest and transparent with parents regarding all policies, information and concerns regarding their children. Parents must be notified if a condition exists that may affect their children's health, mental health and/or safety, including a change to their child's identity.

- I agree that children's innocence should be protected, and schools should be vigilant in guarding children from threats, predatory behavior, and trafficking.

- I agree that parents should have complete access to all student files and records—formal, informal, electronic format and/or hard copy—and that parents should be regularly and fully informed about their child's academic progress, behavioral issues and activities at school.

- I agree that parents should have access to their child's classroom curricula as well as academic, special and alternative programs available to their children at school; that school curricula should be age-appropriate and free from political or ideological indoctrination; and that parents should have the ability to opt their children out of classroom assignments, curricula, and surveys that they deem inappropriate for their children.

- I agree that parents have the right to redress when their rights and their children's rights are violated; the right to express their concerns about their child's curricula or school environment to school officials; and the right to be free from intimidation, harassment and retaliation by teachers, school administrators, school board members or other California elected officials.

Half of the 50 States Have Ditched the NSBA for Targeting Parents

Nebraska joined the ranks of states cutting ties with the National School Boards Association (NSBA) in June 2022, making it the 25th state to boycott the organization after the NSBA sent a letter to President Joe Biden in September 2021 urging the federal government to use domestic terrorism laws to go after parents at school board meetings. The Nebraska Association of School Boards voted to withdraw less than a month after its executive committee voted to cancel its membership, the *Omaha World Herald* reported.

The NSBA's letter to President Biden has enraged half of the states in the union now by suggesting that parental involvement in school board meetings amounts to "domestic terrorism" and by calling on the FBI, the Department of Homeland Security, and the U.S. Secret Service to quash parent interference. The letter's first draft apparently included a petition for use of the Army National Guard but a different copy was sent.

"With such acute threats and actions that are disruptive to our students' well-being, to the safety of public school officials and personnel, and to interstate commerce, we urge the federal government's intervention against individuals or hate groups who are targeting our schools and educators," the letter read.

The only supposed "hate" group referenced in the letter was one that posted watchlists about school boards.

As states like Missouri, Ohio, and Pennsylvania began to drop out of the association almost immediately, the NSBA issued an apology for the letter in October 2021, but the public backtracking hasn't stopped the mass exodus.

Nebraska politicians joined the state school board association in criticism of the NSBA letter, with Sen. Ben Sasse labeling the NSBA's collusion with the Biden Justice Department a "political hack job" and Gov. Pete Ricketts insisting that following the letter's requests would be an "absolute outrageous abuse of federal power" meant to "browbeat parents into not going to school board meetings."

PACS Are Funding 'Parents' Rights Advocates Running for Local School Board Positions

Across the country, new right-leaning political action committees are pouring money into school board races, aiming to flip control of who governs schools in favor of parents rights advocates in a way that rivals the role that teachers unions have historically had in these contests.

For much less than what it would cost them to influence a seat in the House or Senate, these PACs are putting thousands of dollars at a time— sometimes just hundreds—into races for local school boards and as a result, changing education on a national scale.

A super PAC called the 1776 Project PAC is leading the way, emphasizing opposition to lessons related to racial and social justice. With a war chest smaller than what some congressional candidates in competitive districts are raising, the group has supported and opposed school board candidates in a dozen states.

Political action committees, or PACs, and super PACs pool donations from many different people and entities and use that money to try to elect candidates who represent their interests. They may be registered at the federal or state level.

Other PACs are focusing on specific states and races and the candidates with the most money in their campaign accounts tend to be the ones who win. At the school board level, that effect has the potential to be larger because the races are often so cheap.

In a 2018 survey by the National School Boards Association, 75 percent of respondents said they spent less than $1,000 on their election; 16 percent said they spent between $1,000 and $5,000; and only 9 percent said they spent more than $5,000. Most stayed in their positions for long periods of time, and most were volunteers. A recent study from the group School Board Partners showed a changing picture.

Half of the money the 1776 Project PAC has raised—$1.5 million out of $3 million—came from people giving less than $200, according to Federal Election Commission (FEC) filings. Ryan Girdusky, the group's founder, pointed to the more than 40,000 people who have donated to his PAC.

The rise of groups such as the 1776 Project PAC have the potential to outflank local teachers unions, whose endorsements and local funding have been the longtime keys to success in school board races across the country.

A study published in January 2022 by Hoover fellow Michael Hartney at Stanford University showed that "teachers' unions reliably win 70 percent of the school board races in which they make an endorsement." That's the same success rate that the 1776 Project PAC advertises now.

At the local level, PACs and other interest groups are getting involved in ways that have never been seen before and you can get more bang for your buck with these races and win.

In 2022, Moms for Liberty Florida, gave $250 donations to 56 candidates running in 24 county districts, according to records with the Florida Department of Elections. Moms for Liberty Florida was initially funded by Julie Fancelli, heiress to the Publix super markets fortune.

Many of the 56 candidate won elections early this year, and a remaining few are going on to runoff races Nov. 8, 2022, Moms for Liberty co-founder Tiffany Justice said.

The group's Florida-based PAC is funding candidates that "respect fundamental parental rights," Justice said. The term, she explained, is a catch-all for any candidate that does not want to "co-parent with the government."

The Parents' Revolt

Since its inception at the turn of the twentieth century, the Progressive movement has seen the public school system as a potent tool for its political ambitions. Writing in 1930, progressive theorist John Dewey derided the pedagogy of his day as narrow-minded and visionless, arguing that "the traditional schools have almost wholly evaded consideration of the social potentialities of education."

But that was "no reason why progressive schools should continue the evasion," he continued. Instead, he wrote in a subsequent essay, schools should "take an active part in directing social change and share in the construction of a new social order;" progressives should "make the schools their ally," encouraging "the youth who go forth from the schools to take part in the great work of construction and organization that will have to be done."

That activist orientation toward education—in which educators mold students into "agents of change"—radicalized with the rise of the neo-Marxist "critical pedagogy" movement in the late 1960s.

Paulo Freire's *Pedagogy of the Oppressed* (1968), largely credited as critical pedagogy's founding document, called for "a pedagogy which must be forged with, not for, the oppressed," making "oppression and its causes objects of reflection by the oppressed."

Only then, Freire wrote, would beleaguered subjects be capable of "their necessary engagement in the struggle for their liberation." Moving beyond Dewey's reformism, Freire saw education as a way to propagate a revolutionary consciousness—a "process of permanent liberation," through which "the culture of domination is culturally confronted . . . through the change in the way the oppressed perceive the world of oppression" and "the expulsion of the myths created and developed in the old order, which like specters haunt the new structure emerging from the revolutionary transformation."

In other words: critical pedagogy seeks the radical delegitimization of existing institutions and mores, encouraging students to be actively hostile toward everything about the society that they inherit.

Freire's ideas now pervade American education.

"Since the publication of the English edition in 1970, *Pedagogy of the Oppressed* has achieved near-iconic status in America's teacher-training programs," Sol Stern wrote in a 2009 *City Journal* essay.

In 2003, David Steiner and Susan Rozen published a study examining the curricula of 16 schools of education—14 of them among the top-ranked institutions in the country, according to *U.S. News & World Report*—and found that *Pedagogy of the Oppressed* was one of the most frequently assigned texts in their philosophy of education courses."

For the past half-century, the culture war has been less a battle of equals than a story of David and Goliath, in part due to Freire's ideas that now pervade American education and teacher pedagogy. From same-sex marriage to school prayer, the appetite for social transformation unleashed in the 1960s has grown in power with every victory. "History" was supposed to move in only one direction, with the advocates of liberation confident that they were on the right side.

So the fierceness of the recent backlash to CRT and gender ideology in schools took the public education bureaucracy by surprise. The parental uprisings were the bill coming due for the activist agenda that had swept through public education in recent years.

As the Black Lives Matter movement marched through American life in 2020, school boards—already dominated by progressives—redoubled their commitments to the most extreme pedagogical concepts involving race and gender, without pausing to consult parents.

In response, parents across the country began emerging as a formidable political force.

Moms and dads suddenly were signing petitions, holding protests, and demanding answers from a school system grown accustomed to operating without parental scrutiny. In lieu of bake sales and library drives, parents were pulling together to lobby for curricular change.

Some, like Tiffany Justice, even ran for school board seats themselves. Justice, a mother of four, originally won a seat on Florida's Indian River County school board in 2016, well before the current school battles.

Justice's struggle against the education system was initially just about basic quality-of-life issues.

But Justice soon "got a real look at what happens" in local school bureaucracies: "Oftentimes the people who worked within the district or ran the school board had all these relationships that kept them from doing what was best for kids. I would go into the executive bargaining sessions, and the teachers' union would bargain for the teachers. The district would bargain for the district system. Who was bargaining for the parents and the kids?"

In January 2021, Justice cofounded Moms for Liberty, with Tina Descovich, another mother serving on a school board in a neighboring county. The 501 (c) 4 "started with two chapters—one in my county, one in Tina's county," Justice says. "Within three weeks, we had a call from Nassau, New York—it was a Long Island mom who called us and said, 'I want to start a Moms for Liberty chapter.'"

For decades, American public education had continued to press left, largely without organized opposition.

But in 2020, something broke. That year, "two simultaneous phenomena occurred," Christopher F. Rufo says. "First, you had the pandemic, which shut down schools and made classrooms virtual, so parents could have a really close look at what was being transmitted to their kids."

And second, he continues, "after the death of George Floyd, you had this universal spasm through all of our institutions, which were tripping over themselves trying to adopt the left-wing racial ideology. A lot of these more radical educators—whether they're in the Diversity, Equity and Inclusion departments of K–12 public schools, or actually in the classroom—saw that as their greatest opportunity in decades to start promoting those left-wing racialist ideologies throughout the education system." Parents "hit the panic button," says Rufo.

Justice agrees. "During Covid, we saw an expert class that failed us," she says. "It's very hard when you're a parent, and you've chosen a direction for your child's education, to admit that what you've chosen isn't working.

But parents, all of a sudden, saw all of these people whom they had trusted failing their kids. And then they were emboldened to ask more questions."

The parents' movement had another powerful tool at its disposal: social media.

Videos of parents giving impassioned speeches at school board meetings routinely went viral starting in 2021. One Virginia mother, Stacy Langton, was banned from her district's school library after she was shown, in a widely circulated video, confronting the Fairfax County school board over the presence of the sexually explicit graphic novel *Gender Queer* on the library's shelves.

But the district's harsh crackdown against Langton only served to make her—and the movement she represented—more sympathetic. "The only weapon I have at my disposal, to try to force them to do the right thing, is to continue to apply the pressure publicly," Langton tells me. "And that's the thing I think that parents need to take from my example and the example of other parents who have gone to these school board meetings.

There's so much value in simply showing up and saying your piece— because look at what's happened since last September 2021. Who would have thought, when I went there on September 23, that we would be having a national conversation about gender ideology in schools six or eight months later?"

These days, Langton says, "parents randomly reach out to me on X (formerly Twitter). I get so many comments and remarks from parents all over the country that they're more awake about this issue now than they were even last fall." People regularly send her videos of other parents who brought Gender Queer to their school board meetings. "Other parents are taking the baton and running with it," Langton observes, "and they have the courage now to speak up."

At least 17 states have passed restrictions on the teaching of CRT-based concepts in public schools; others are expected to follow suit this legislative session. Some states, including Florida, have also passed bills cracking down on the teaching of radical sexual and gender ideology in the classroom.

School board recalls hit an all-time high in 2021, according to Ballotpedia.

That dissatisfaction has even reached deep-blue areas like San Francisco, where voters recalled three school board members by landslide margins in February 2022.

The institutional conservative world has also coalesced around the parents' agenda: think tanks (including *City Journal*'s publisher, the Manhattan Institute) are producing model legislation for CRT bans (as previously noted and listed in the Appendix), sending scholars to testify before state legislatures on the topic, and committing resources to bridging the gap between the Beltway and the grassroots.

In December 2021, Christopher F. Rufo helped The Heritage Foundation produce a mission statement of sorts for the parents' movement, signed by numerous heavy-hitters in the world of conservative education policy. "The entire movement has shifted in the last two years," says Rufo.

"Critical race theory provides us with what I believe is the proof of concept and the political model for how to fight these fights. At the beginning, when I was first reporting on CRT and working on the activism side of the issue, a lot of the more establishment political and intellectual figures were hesitant. But if you fast-forward a year, pretty much the entire movement is on board."

At the legislative level, rising Republican stars like Florida governor Ron DeSantis have cut their teeth on the school issue. DeSantis broke through with conservatives during the pandemic, when he made the difficult decision to force school districts to reopen, over the objections of unions, many health officials, and the national media.

As the pandemic subsided, and the debates over curricular issues emerged, the governor passed an aggressive slate of bills addressing everything from CRT and gender ideology to viewpoint diversity, civics education, and parental rights.

"In part what elevated it was parents bringing this forward, saying, 'this was in my child's textbook,' or 'my child's teacher wrote these odd things on the whiteboard,'" an official in DeSantis's office explains.

"We started asking about what avenues we had to investigate this because first off, a lot of this content, just historically, it's fiction. Second, it's a very indoctrinating—kind of brainwashing—type of curriculum. And third, it's taking away time from the curriculum standards that schools are required to teach."

Complaint after complaint came in, the official says—"from districts, from different schools, and from teachers themselves, saying, 'I'm not comfortable teaching this. I know it's fiction. I know it's not accurate. Why am I being told to teach this?'"

Other states have followed suit.

In Texas, Governor Greg Abbott signed laws aimed at combating CRT and renewing civics education in public classrooms, and Lieutenant Governor Dan Patrick has made a ban on instruction surrounding sexual and gender ideology—akin to Florida's hotly debated Parental Rights in Education Bill—a "top priority" for the next legislative session.

States such as Alabama have already passed laws aimed at combating gender ideology in public schools. South Carolina governor Henry McMaster launched "a comprehensive investigation into the presence of obscene and pornographic materials in public schools in South Carolina."

And Republicans like Glenn Youngkin have run and won on the curriculum issue. In 2021, the gubernatorial candidate staged an upset victory in typically blue Virginia by tapping a reservoir of parental dissatisfaction, polling ahead of his Democratic opponent among parents of K–12 students by nearly 20 points in the lead-up to the election.

Public opinion appears firmly with the Right in these debates.

Florida's parental rights bill, dubbed the "Don't Say Gay" law by critics, is favored by 16 points by registered voters nationwide. According to YouGov, Americans who have heard of CRT disagree that it "is something students should be exposed to in school" by 14 points.

But the education bureaucracy won't go down without a fight despite the election upsets and the parents' movement has been widely denigrated in the liberal media outlets, decried by local and national politicians alike, and attacked by a constellation of powerful institutions.

The National School Boards Association even asked the Biden administration in a letter to "examine appropriate enforceable actions" against school board protesters under the PATRIOT Act in September 2021. (An earlier draft of the letter requested that "the Army National Guard and its Military Police be deployed to certain school districts and related events where students and school personnel have been subjected to acts and threats of violence.")

Some parents, like Rhode Island's Nicole Solas, have been targeted by teachers' unions. The stay-at-home mother is battling a lawsuit filed against her by the Rhode Island chapter of the National Education Association in response to open-records requests that she filed to learn more about the content of her children's education.

Particularly in blue states like Rhode Island, parents face an array of social and institutional pressures. "People send me screenshots of people bad-mouthing me online, in my town," Solas tells me. "My town is extremely liberal and in a very liberal state. But I do have a lot of allies. You would never know it, because of the politics of the town. But people are really determined to get common-sense candidates in school board seats."

"The battle for the classroom matters; it is a microcosm of questions at the root of our political divisions."

Taking an incremental approach, parents like Solas and her many counterparts are reclaiming American schools.

Debates over education policy, traditionally organized around technocratic issues like public funding and school choice, have become a proxy for the nation's broader cultural fissures—the teaching of American history, the meaning of gender, the rights of parents and families, and traditional American notions of "equality" versus a race-conscious vision of "equity."

The Left's treatment of the classroom debate is characterized by a fundamental antipathy to the traditional family. McAuliffe's dismissal of the idea that parents should have a say in their children's education has long been a feature of progressive political philosophy. Back in 2013, an MSNBC promotional video featured one of the network's hosts denouncing "our kind of private idea that kids belong to their parents, or kids belong to their families."

In a 2021 op-ed for the *Washington Post*—titled "Parents Claim They Have the Right to Shape Their Kids' School Curriculum. They Don't"—two education-policy writers worried: "To turn over all decisions to parents . . . would risk inhibiting the ability of young people to think independently." Speaking at a teachers' conference earlier this year, Joe Biden declared: "They're all our children. . . . They're not somebody else's children; they're like yours when they're in the classroom."

The Right has a historic opportunity to position itself as the "parents' party."

The parents' movement is driven by the most powerful impulse of all: a desire to protect one's children. As long as progressives are unwilling even to recognize the existence of a cultural problem in their approach to the classroom, they will continue to drive away the millions of working- and middle-class parents who may not think of themselves as conservative in the traditional sense but are repelled by college campus–style wokeness; indignant at critical race theory, gender ideology, and anti-Americanism in their children's schools; and suspicious of the Left's radically ambitious social-engineering schemes.

In this sense, the political earthquake in public education contains the seeds of national renewal. The art of self-government is no easy task; good citizenship must be taught. For most of our history, the education system was organized around teaching young Americans a love of justice, an understanding of the distinction between liberty and license, and a sense of patriotic duty. There's no reason that this cannot be our future, too— across the country, mothers and fathers are demanding as much. We should listen.

7 –Parental Rights, Books Bans & Left-Leaning ALA

Credit: Boston Globe via Getty Images–Drag Queen Story Hour.

The issue of parents' rights is among the most heated in public education, invoked in political campaigns and debates over everything from COVID policy and curriculum choices to classroom discussions about race, gender, and sexuality.

Most recently, the principle has been a potent rallying cry for conservative activists and politicians, including Virginia's Republican Gov. Glenn Youngkin in his winning gubernatorial campaign. But the concept is tangled in more than a century of legal wrangling, court precedents, federal and state statutes, and rhetoric over what it actually means, especially in education.

"People who invoke the term 'parental rights' have different things in mind and different aspirations," said Neal McCluskey, the director of the Center for Educational Freedom at the libertarian Cato Institute in Washington. "My general impression when I see people invoking 'parental rights,' it's been connected to a general idea that parents have been cut out of decisions made by schools."

Jeffrey Shulman, a visiting professor at Georgetown University Law Center and the author of several law journal articles on parental rights, said he agrees the term "is thrown about loosely" and could refer to rights under the U.S. Constitution, under federal statutes, under state constitutions or state statutes, or even school board regulations.

"Generally speaking, when parents use the term in the heat of battle, they are pretty much calling upon some amorphous, free-floating right," Shulman said.

The arguments advanced by some conservative parents today reflect a longstanding and deep-seated fear, he said, "that our system of public education indoctrinates children in a left-wing ideological agenda; that public schools alienate children from their families and cultures, thereby undermining parental authority; [and] that, basically, the goal of public education is to enlist children on the wrong side of our current culture wars."

"These arguments should not be dismissed out of hand," Shulman added. "But much of what we're seeing in the news is outright hostility to any form of common education."

Moms for Liberty advocate sees at least some common ground.

That's certainly not how some parental-rights advocates on the conservative side view things.

Tiffany Justice, a co-founder of the group Moms for Liberty, which has grown quickly as a major voice for parental rights since being founded in 2021, is quick to point out that she served on her local school board, in Florida's Indian River County. The mother of four school-aged children worked on such mundane issues as school start times. (She tried to make them later.)

"We support public education," said Justice. "But we have an education system that is failing parents."

Moms for Liberty was formed in early 2021 in Florida and now has nearly 250 chapters in 42 states. The group pushed for parental rights statutes passed in the state in 2021 and 2022.

The 2022 law, called the Florida Parental Rights in Education Act, prohibits classroom instruction about sexual orientation or gender identity in K-3 classrooms, and requires such conversations after 3rd grade to be age-appropriate, which the state board of education has yet to define. The measure has been derided by opponents as the "Don't Say Gay" law and has been challenged in court.

The measure, which built on a 2021 state law called the Florida Parents' Bill of Rights, also requires that parents be notified about health-care services offered at the child's school, with the right to decline any service offered. And the law requires parental approval for questionnaires or health screenings given to K-3 students.

Florida's recent laws address "the audacity of the teachers and some bureaucrats to think they know better" than parents what is best for students, Justice said.

Justice now travels the country speaking in favor of similar legislation. Some 26 states are considering legislation this year that would expand parental rights in education, according to FutureEd, a think tank at Georgetown University's McCourt School of Public Policy.

Justice pushed back at the idea that her group is responsible for sowing division in public schools. "I think we have much more in common with most parents than people think," she said.

The ALA Twists the Meaning of "Book Ban"

Critics say the ALA is behind the movement to make the country's libraries centers of wokeness. What's being removed from school libraries is material entirely inappropriate for students. Warning, examples below!

The Left has been collectively hyperventilating about "book bans" for months. No one should be surprised that liberals are redefining the word "ban" in an effort to stigmatize conservative politicians leading the movement for parental rights in education. But some moderate Republicans have also signaled that they, too, buy into the idea that restricting content based on age-appropriateness constitutes a "book ban."

The first definition of the word "banned" in the Merriam-Webster dictionary is "to prohibit especially by legal means." So when Americans hear claims from the Left that, say, Florida governor Ron DeSantis is "banning books," they often incorrectly take those words at face value, assuming that the books have been removed not just from school libraries but also public libraries and bookstores.

I live in Florida and recently tested the availability of six well-known "banned" books that have been removed from some school libraries here. I had no trouble getting any of them at my public library—but I was shocked that anyone would purchase books with such graphic adult content for a school library.

The influential Kirkus Reviews hailed George Johnson's *All Boys Aren't Blue*, for example, as "a critical, captivating, merciful mirror for growing up Black and queer today." But the book's depictions of sex acts are pornographic. Consider these passages from chapter 15 (you may want to skip to the next paragraph):

I put some lube on and got him up on his knees, and I began to slide into him from behind. . . .

I pulled out of him and kissed him while he masturbated. . . . He asked me to turn over while he slipped a condom on himself. . . . This was my ass, and I was struggling to imagine someone inside me. . . . he got on top and slowly inserted himself into me. It was the worst pain I think I have ever felt in my life. . . . eventually I felt a mix of pleasure with the pain.

Meantime, Penguin Random House, along with a coalition of lefty groups, sued Florida's Escambia County for removing inappropriate books from its school libraries. One of the "banned" books the publisher mentions in the suit is Toni Morrison's *The Bluest Eye*. The novel is full of adult themes like rape and incest that most parents wouldn't want their children exposed to. Here's a graphic example (and the same warning applies):

His memories of Pauline and the doing of a wild and forbidden thing excited him and a bolt of desire ran down his genitals, giving it length and softening the lips of his anus. Surrounding all of this lust was a border of politeness.

He wanted to f*ck her tenderly, but the tenderness would not hold. The tightness of her vagina was more than he could bear.

PolitiFact recently fact-checked DeSantis's claim that no books have been banned in Florida. They rated his statements false—not misleading or partly true or needing context—because the American Library Association (ALA) and other left-leaning groups define the word banned in a much broader way than the commonsense definition. The ALA defines a ban as "the removal of a book based on a person or group's objection."

According to a recent report cited in the *Wall Street Journal*, a total of 1,269 book challenges were filed at libraries (public and school) nationwide in 2022. With more than 117,000 libraries in the U.S., this means that less than 1 percent of libraries received even a single challenge.

The ALA Has Long Been Notoriously Liberal—and Now Woke

Libraries, for decades the ultimate safe spaces, have become ground zero in the ongoing culture wars, with battles over banned books, drag queen story hours, and free access to porn raging all over the country.

The newly-elected head of the ALA—a self-described "Marxist lesbian" named Emily Drabinski said, "So many of us find ourselves at the ends of our worlds," during her campaign to become ALA president. "The consequences of decades of unchecked climate change, class war, white supremacy, and imperialism have led us here. If we want a world that includes public goods like the library, we must organize our collective power and wield it. The American Library Association offers us a set of tools that can harness our energies and build those capacities."

"The average person has no idea of this but librarians have been targeting children in recent years and trying to turn them into political activists," said Dan Kleinman, a self-described "library watchdog" from Chatham, New Jersey, who has run a website called "Safe Libraries" for more than 10 years. He said he has documented the alarming radicalization of the nation's libraries, including what he says is readily available porn in library computers.

Drag Queen Story Hour, which was launched in San Francisco in 2015, has become a mainstay for children at libraries all over the US and the UK. Drag queens in full regalia perform for children as young as two and three. Though at least two registered sex offenders were found to have been among the drag queens performing at a Houston public library in 2019, the program is still going strong.

A recent IPSOS/NPR poll indicates that the media has been highly effective in distorting the truth about book-banning in the U.S. and obscuring the graphic content of titles removed from school libraries. According to the survey, only 41 percent of Republicans strongly or somewhat support school boards "banning" certain books. (The figure is just 21 percent overall.)

Biden's Justice Department branded parents who complained about inappropriate books in their children's school libraries "domestic terrorist" threats.

The conservative biased Southern Poverty Law Center (SPLC) and other left-wing groups have labeled Moms for Liberty and other groups supporting parental rights in education as "extremist" groups. And the administration recently announced the hiring of a book ban coordinator to work in the Department of Education's Office for Civil Rights.

In his campaign-launch video, Biden lamented that Republicans are "banning books," and as he spoke those words, a copy of *To Kill a Mockingbird* was prominently placed atop a stack of books. But in a fact check last year, even the Associated Press, which is aggressively hostile to DeSantis, has acknowledged that the book was never banned in Florida. It has been pulled from libraries and curriculums in various places—nearly all of them liberal enclaves, like Burbank, California, Madison, Wisconsin, and Seattle.

The Left and apparently now some Republicans as well believe that parents should not question curation decisions made by public school librarians. They want the state to be free to indoctrinate young people. According to an analysis of campaign donations by Zippia, 91 percent of political contributions from library directors went to Democrats in the last election cycle, and this dynamic hasn't changed in years. A 2005 article in the Chronicle of Higher Education noted that, in the preceding year, librarians donated to John Kerry over George W. Bush by a ratio of 223 to one.

In fact, progressive librarians already practice a form of book banning by not ordering books seen as "conservative," ordering very few copies of them, or not featuring them prominently compared with liberal titles. For example, the public library system in Pinellas County, where I live, owns no copies of *Johnny the Walrus*, a children's book by Daily Wire contributor Matt Walsh, though it has nearly 8,000 reviews on Amazon and a 4.9-star average rating. But the system has seven copies of *Let's Talk About It*, a graphic novel by Erika Moen and Matthew Nolan featuring sexually explicit images and themes, as well as copies of every other prominently "banned" young adult book.

Just as conservatives have gained traction on gender identity by asking leftists to define the word "woman," they could also reframe the book debate by asking them to define the word "ban." They shouldn't let the Left avoid acknowledging the explicit or graphic content of many of these books, and they should ask defenders of these titles whether they want their own children reading them. When movies and television programs are rated PG–13, R, or X—and consequently restricted for younger viewers—that doesn't mean that they're banned. The same principle goes for books.

Assaults on Parental Rights

"Dangerous." "Offensive." "Discrimination."

New Jersey leftwing Attorney General Matt Platkin threw those words around in a recent interview as he attacked parents who are standing up for their rights in public schools. But it's not just words. AG Platkin recently sued to stop parents from finding out what's going on inside those schools, and he is going to extremes to stand between parents and their children. But the Goldwater Institute is fighting back on parents' behalf in New Jersey and around the country, because parental rights aren't "dangerous"—they're a fundamental, constitutionally protected liberty.

Several New Jersey school boards adopted policies earlier this year to keep parents informed about changes in their children's gender identity. After all, parents should be involved in important decisions involving minors. AG Platkin responded by suing the school boards for "discrimination." That's when the Goldwater Institute stepped in on behalf of a New Jersey mom of two, reminding the court that public schools are constitutionally required to keep parents informed about what's happening to their kids in school

Now, AG Platkin is taking his assault on parental rights to the airwaves.

"I do think some things around these boards are being fueled by the national and state political dialogue," he said in a recent radio interview. "It's a dialogue that I think is dangerous. Again, I just find it offensive," he added, before claiming that the parental notification policies "target our kids…to score cheap political points."

Dangerous? Never mind that AG Platkin conveniently neglected to mention that the parental notification policies include built-in safeguards to ensure each situation is dealt with on a case-by-case basis and to balance a student's needs with a parent's rights.

Offensive? No, what's offensive is keeping secrets from parents about their own children's wellbeing. What's offensive is the government attempting to replace parents as the primary raisers of kids. As Middletown mom of three Caterina Skalaski told the *New York Post*. "I do not, will not ever co-parent with the government."

Cheap political points? Tell that to the 77 percent of New Jerseyans who think schools should keep parents informed about changes in their children's gender identity. Tell it to concerned Middletown mom Laura Abt. "Everyone says this is a political battle between the left and the right. I'm not a political activist. I'm a mother trying to protect my two kids," she says, "This isn't anti-trans legislation. This is about parents' rights." (AG Platkin also failed to mention that he sent his lawyers to court to sue one school district less than 48 hours after the district adopted a parental notification policy! Talk about cheap political points.)

Or tell it to Amber Lavigne, a Maine mom whose rights Goldwater is defending after a school social worker encouraged her 13-year-old daughter in her gender transition, gave the child a chest-binder, and advised the student not to tell her parents. That mom, Amber, isn't even a conservative; she's a socially liberal registered Democrat who calls herself "a pretty open-minded person." Yet Amber also says that ordeal has "ripped my family apart."

One more thing: AG Platkin claims he's in the right because the "law is the law." But the highest law of the land, the U.S. Constitution, protects parents' right to stay informed. In fact, both the U.S. and New Jersey Supreme Courts have consistently upheld parents' fundamental right to control and direct the education, upbringing, and healthcare decisions of their children. But in order to meaningfully exercise that right, parents must be told when the government, including public school officials, make decisions that directly affect their children's mental health or physical well-being.

In other words, the Constitution requires transparency, not secrecy.

But public school secrecy goes beyond gender transitions, too. In states like Rhode Island and Texas, Goldwater is helping concerned parents get the answers they deserve after school districts charged them thousands of dollars in public records fees to find out what's going on in their kids' schools.

Governments across the nation have launched an assault on the very concept of parenting, and on every single parent who dares to ask what's going on in their children's school.

It needs to end. They're not the government's kids.

Parents' Bill of Rights Can Help State School Reformers

Parents and schools are supposed to be partners, not rivals—and in that relationship, it's moms and dads who are the senior partners. The contempt for parents' rights has fueled a long train of abuses, from racist curricula to a war on girls sports and bathrooms to...criminal cover-ups.

Failing such minimal conditions of parental trust and student well-being is not education or even activism. It's something more like child abuse. Furthermore, good principals, teachers, and school boards want parents involved. They want parents to know what books their kids are reading and what's being taught.

Nonetheless, the stunning success of conservative education reform across the country in the past few years is the result a moral fact: Parents are children's primary educators. Until very recently, this was not disputed, let alone controversial.

But lately, it has become clear that progressive elites who run teachers unions and school boards, the Democratic Party, and the corporate media no longer share this view. Their contempt for parents' rights has fueled a long train of abuses, from racist curricula to a war on girls sports and bathrooms to darker episodes of criminal cover-ups and student grooming.

The good news is, conservative leaders have answered this challenge with action, rather than just tweets and talking points. The better news is, it has been elected conservatives in the states leading and delivering substantive K-12 policy reforms.

Fifteen states have already adopted Parents' Bill of Rights laws that affirm moms and dads as the ultimate authority on their kids' education. Lawmakers in a dozen other states are considering similar proposals this year.

Some governors, such as Florida's Ron DeSantis, have gone even further, asserting authority over public education in their states to, among other things, rid school libraries of pornographic books and classrooms of "woke" indoctrination.

An additional 11 states have passed transparency reforms that give parents access to public schools' instructional materials. And at least four more may follow their lead in 2023 and beyond.

To the Left, these are political encroachments into a space that belongs exclusively to trained, licensed, unionized Marxist activists. To everyone else, this stuff is common sense.

Of course parents should be able to see what their kids are being taught in schools. Of course public schools should not be shelving porn, staging sexually explicit performances, or forcing children to sit through lessons that conflict with their family's values. Of course the bigotry and superstitions of "critical theory" have no place in elementary school classrooms. And of course school employees should not hide—let alone encourage—children's mental health challenges behind parents' backs.

Failing such minimal conditions of parental trust and student well-being is not education or even activism. It's something more like child abuse.

As conservatives around the country lead this fight, conservatives in Congress are wondering how Washington can help. The first thing they can do—on education, as in so many other areas—is to wield the power they have.

For too long, conservatives—either out of aversion to conflict or lack of imagination—have shied away from using the authority voters give them to win real victories against the Left.

This is not to say that Republicans should seek a federal takeover of public education the next time they control Congress and the White House. Rather, conservatives should identify the nexuses between institutions they control and the problems American families face—and act.

The Parents' Bill of Rights Act, introduced in the U.S. House of Representatives by Rep. Julia Letlow, R-La., and 122 co-sponsors, puts a bright spotlight on the importance of transparency to parents. It clarifies for confused school boards and woke administrators that their federal funds are predicated on serving their students, parents, and communities—not their ideology.

The bill would require federally supported schools to post or distribute their curricula, and to make both their budgets and classroom materials available to students' parents. It guarantees parents' right to speak at school board meetings, meet with their children's teachers, and be appraised of disciplinary and academic issues.

Kevin D. Roberts, Ph.D, a fifth-generation educator himself, says, "These are practices good schools already do. Good principals, teachers, and school boards want parents involved. They want parents to know what books their kids are reading and what's being taught in their classrooms."

Importantly, the proposal offers needed improvements to the Family Educational Rights and Privacy Act, including provisions that prohibit schools from acting as a student's parent when it comes to technology usage, along with prohibitions on school officials making decisions for a child on vaccines. The proposal also blocks the sale of student information for commercial purposes. These would be welcome updates to federal law.

Parents and schools are supposed to be partners, not rivals—and in that relationship, it's moms and dads who are the senior partners. That's the principle that should guide conservative education reformers at every level of government.

For cities and counties, that means choosing curricula that reflect communities' goals and values. For states, that means protecting children's innocence and privacy, protecting parents' authority over their kids (including via school choice), and protecting everyone from bigotry, idiocy, and propaganda at school.

Finally, for Congress, that means reminding all Americans that when it comes to education, government works for moms, dads, and kids—not the other way around.

The Pennsbury School Board voted July 13, 2022 to settle a free speech lawsuit that gained national attention after they were caught editing public comments from the March 2021 and May 2021 meetings.

The school board voted to settle the lawsuit brought forward by Lower Makefield Township residents Tim Daly, Simon Campbell, Doug Marshall, and Robert Abrams. The four said Pennsbury and several of their officials violated their First Amendment rights by cutting them off, not allowing their comments, and editing their statements from video recordings of school board meetings.

The settlement agreement, which is being paid for by the district's insurance company, will pay $237,590 to the Institute for Free Speech, which represented the men; $62,410 to Montgomery County, Pennsylvania law firm Vangrossi & Rechuitti; and $17.91 to each of the four plaintiffs for damages.

The Institute for Free Speech said in a statement the $17.91 in damages was a symbolic gesture to mark the year the First Amendment was ratified. For a video of the incident, follow the link in the Appendix.

8 – Reversing America's 'D -' Grade Education System to an Ascendant 'A +' Grade

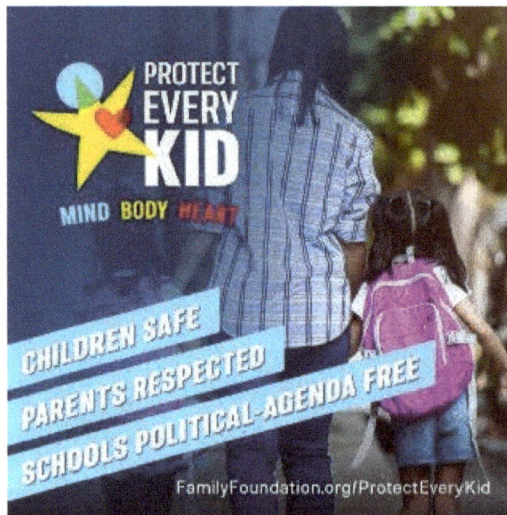

Credit: The Family Foundation–Parents' Bill of Rights.

America is finally waking up to the fact that poisonous, divisive ideas are proliferating in public education, from pre-K to graduate school. The question is how to push back against such ideas, and recognize the damage that is being done to young minds. We must never downplay how serious this issue is as we consider another frightening quote, this one from Vladimir Lenin: "Give me four years to teach the children and the seed I have sown will never be uprooted."

Solutions are easier in K-12; primary and secondary teachers do not have the same protections of academic freedom that college faculty have, and the K-12 curriculum is more tightly controlled by state agencies. The issue is more complex in academia, where academic freedom reigns and the curriculum is controlled by a decentralized faculty.

The situation is also more dire at the college level: Higher education is where the bad ideas originate, and, for a long time, academia has seen little opposition to radicalization of public universities. While boards of trustees have the legal right to control curricula, they have almost universally relinquished that power to the faculty in practice.

In recent years, however, with the degradation of much of the academy reaching an advanced stage, state legislatures have begun to rise to the challenge and push back against radical encroachment on the public-college curriculum.

The Pushback Against Classroom Indoctrination Begins

One such attempt is Florida's "Stop the Wrongs to Our Kids and Employees (WOKE) Act." This 2022 law statutorily prohibits discriminatory classroom teaching. It targets such divisive ideas as Critical Race Theory (CRT), which demands that members of a racial group must perpetually atone for injustices committed by members of their group centuries before, and that claims by aggrieved minorities against the offending groups should pass unchallenged.

It should be obvious that such a system of preferences and punishments along racial and ethnic lines will make a pluralistic society such as the United States unworkable without oppressive government control. Simply accepting the status quo of this biased indoctrination is no longer acceptable to the majority of Americans who, as taxpayers, provide many of the funds for public universities. Thus, the situation screams for reform.

But not everybody wants that reform, and the Stop Woke Act is a point of departure from many long-established academic practices. As can be expected, the law has received a hailstorm of criticism from faculty and civil-rights organizations that favor the status quo. A rapidly filed lawsuit intended to render the law unconstitutional was thrown out of a U.S. district court because the plaintiffs lacked the necessary "standing."

Much of the criticism depends on a fundamentally incorrect assumption about who "owns" the public universities and is therefore in charge of institutional policies such as who decides what and how to teach. Many academics and their supporters claim that higher education belongs to the faculty, deriving this notion of ownership from the formation of medieval universities in Northern Europe (especially England) as "guilds" of faculty.

Florida Parents Take Back the Classroom

"It is a fundamental right of parents to direct the upbringing, education, and care of their minor children." That's the opening line of Florida's Parents' Bill of Rights, signed into law in June 2021. Similar bills have been proposed in Missouri, Kentucky, Texas, and even at the federal level.

"Our children do not belong to the government," says Patti Sullivan, state coordinator for Parental Rights Florida, which has pushed for legislation of this sort since 2013. But parental rights laws and anti–critical race theory bills can't end the curriculum wars. Only school choice can. "We do not co-parent with the government. And these entities seem to think that they are entitled to our children, and they are not," says Sullivan.

State bans on the teaching of critical race theory (CRT), which have swept the nation, are a more aggressive attempt to limit the discretion that teachers and administrators have over what's taught in school. They've been especially popular with voters.

Republican Glenn Youngkin ousted the heavily favored Terry McAuliffe in the Virginia governor's race after he campaigned against CRT in schools, and on his first day in office, he banned it from classrooms via executive order. Four other states have also banned CRT, and several more are considering similar bills.

However, opponents of CRT bans and more modest bills to force schools to post their curricula online say that "curriculum transparency bills are just thinly veiled attempts at chilling teachers and students from learning and talking about race and gender in schools," as the American Civil Liberties Union recently tweeted.

Parents have never had the "right to shape their kids' school curriculum," authors of a recent *Washington Post* op-ed argued. If that's what parents want, it says, they should opt out and "send their children to private or religious schools."

But why should families who can afford private school be the only ones who have a say in how their children are taught?

"I'm pretty skeptical of the government deciding what should be taught in any type of school," says Corey DeAngelis, national director of research for the American Federation for Children and a senior fellow at Reason Foundation. He says public school parents should also have the right to choose the most fitting academic setting for their kids. The solution is to "fund students, not systems," giving families the choice to spend education dollars on the schooling of their choosing instead of the one-size-fits-all approach offered by traditional public schools.

"[CRT] bills are just a form of whack-a-mole, where your CRT battles of today were the common core battles of yesterday, and it'll be something else going forward because the reality is parents disagree about what kind of education they want their kids to have...And the better solution is the bottom-up accountability in allowing families to vote with their feet," says DeAngelis.

This has become such a hot-button issue because the pandemic gave parents direct exposure to exactly what their children were and weren't being taught.

"Parents are awake now that they have seen the curriculum," says Tina Descovich, a former Brevard County, Florida, school board member and co-founder of Moms for Liberty. "They now understand school district policies, which they had never looked at before. They are understanding the structure, who holds authority, and what types of authority, within the education system. I think that's vital, and it's something that's been lacking for a long time."

Florida Parents' Bill of Rights

In contrast to CRT bans, the Florida Parents' Bill of Rights broadly affirms that parents have a right to know what schools are teaching and providing to their children.

One of the most controversial aspects of the bill is how it applies to medical and mental health services. It establishes that any medical services provided without parental consent can result in misdemeanor charges.

Patti Sullivan says some parents are particularly concerned that schools are counseling their kids on their sexuality and gender identity without parental consent. The parents of one student in a Tallahassee public school sued after the staff held a meeting without their knowledge to discuss accommodating their 13-year-old's shift to a nonbinary gender identity. They also noted in a file that the student's "privacy when [staff are] speaking to parents" must be considered.

"The law states that they must share all information with the parent," says Sullivan. "I think that it's very important that we maintain the fact that these parents are entrusting their children to these [government] entities, and they are not qualified or equipped to make those decisions [regarding sexuality and gender]."

Corey DeAngelis maintains that the clash of values is best addressed through increased school choice.

"We force families into a one-size-fits-all, government-run school system, and these bills try to prohibit or encourage certain types of policies in that one-size-fits-all system," says DeAngelis. "The only way to move forward with freedom rather than force is to allow the money to follow the child to wherever they want to get an education that aligns best with their parents' values."

The pandemic-related school closures have bolstered the school choice movement, with 22 states expanding, improving, or implementing new school choice programs in 2021.

Florida is already far ahead of most states in providing parents with school choice, but DeAngelis says it should go further by offering universal vouchers and education savings accounts, which would truly empower parents and children to opt for any school of their choosing.

"What better way to assert parental rights are important than to empower them directly by allowing the money to follow their child to wherever they get an education? Funding students directly truly empowers parents when it comes to their kid's education. That is the best way to assert those rights," says DeAngelis.

Gov. Youngkin Bans Critical Race Theory, But More Reform is Necessary

The National Association of Scholars (NAS) and the Civics Alliance are delighted that newly inaugurated Virginia Governor Glenn Youngkin has begun his term by declaring that he will make good on his campaign promises. Per their model legislations and recommendations outlined and explained below:

His Executive Order #1 directs the state administration to remove Critical Race Theory (CRT) from the public K-12 schools. His Executive Order #2 directs the state administration to remove the mask mandate from the public K-12 schools. We congratulate Governor Youngkin for moving so swiftly to redeem his promises—and to redeem Virginia's children from the authoritarian whims of the public school bureaucracy.

Yet the state of Virginia must do more, to institutionalize education reform in Virginia. Virginia's education bureaucracy, as education bureaucracies throughout the nation, remains deeply committed to CRT and other radical ideologies. We urge Governor Youngkin to address these priorities during his administration:

PARENTS' RIGHTS: Governor Youngkin rightly stated in his Executive Order #2 that "parents, not the government, have the fundamental right to make decisions concerning the care of their children." Virginia should pass laws that will give parents the power to enforce their rights to determine their children's education. These laws should include:

- An Academic Transparency Act, to require public schools to publicize transparently every category of document relating to schools' policies and procedures.

- A Financial Transparency Act, to require school districts to post immediately on a public website a transparent, detailed financial statement that itemizes all expenditures.

- A School Board Election Date Act, to shift school board election dates to the same day as the general election, and thereby improve education reformers' chances to win school board elections.

- A School Board Member Recall Act, to establish straightforward procedures by which to recall school board members.

Virginia's parents should not need to depend on Virginia's governor to find out what their schools are doing or to remove school board members devoted to indoctrination rather than education. These laws will give Virginia's parents real power to run their schools.

CRITICAL RACE THEORY AND ACTION CIVICS: Governor Youngkin's Executive Order #1 is good within its scope, but it should be expanded to be effective. Virginia should pass laws to remove CRT and Action Civics (which is used to provide vocational training in radical activism) entirely from the state's public K-12 schools. These laws should include:

- A Partisanship Out of Civics Act, to prevent teachers from giving credit to Action Civics or any other sort of public policy advocacy in history, government, civics, or social studies, and to bar civics classes from using the discriminatory ideology at the heart of Critical Race Theory.

- A Classroom Learning Act, to eliminate service-learning pedagogy from public K-12 schools.

- A Values Assessment Act, to prohibit public schools from assessing, rewarding, or punishing students, teachers, or administrators for their level of commitment to any value or attitude.

- A Contractor Nondiscrimination Act, to require contractors for school districts to prohibit the use of Critical Race Theory policies that require discrimination by race, sex, or other group identity.

REFORMED STATE STANDARDS: Radical education bureaucrats impose their ideology by distorting the state education standards as well as by explicit injection of CRT and Action Civics. Virginia should pass laws to restore proper education standards to its public K-12 schools. These laws should include:

- A Social Studies Curriculum Act, to mandate K-12 instruction in Economics, State History, United States History, Civics, and Western Civilization.

- A Civics Course Act, to mandate a year-long high school civics course, including requirements to study the primary documents of the American founding and bans on Action Civics and the components of Critical Race Theory.

- A United States History Act, to mandate a year-long high school United States History course, including requirements to study the primary documents of American history and bans on Action Civics and the components of Critical Race Theory.

- A Western Civilization Act, to mandate a year-long high school Western Civilization course, including requirements to study the primary documents of Western Civilization and bans on Action Civics and the components of Critical Race Theory.

- A Schools Nondiscrimination Act, to mandate that no one should be either included or excluded from our nation's content standards, curricula, trainings, textbooks, and other school materials on account of their race, sex, or other group identity.

- A Historical Documents Act, to mandate instruction in historical documents and the liberty to use historical documents.

- A Legislative Review Act, to require all existing academic standards, and all forthcoming revisions, to be submitted to the state legislature and the governor for review and possible veto.

HIGHER EDUCATION: Radical advocates have also seized control of universities, education schools, and teacher licensure. The campaign against CRT and Action Civics, if it is to succeed, must also include work to reform these institutions. Legislative priorities should include:

- A modified version of the Partisanship Out of Civics Act, to forbid administrative trainings and policies that inculcate CRT, but which incorporates recognition of the constitutionally established sphere of academic freedom in higher education.

- An American History Act, to add an American History and Government general education requirement to public universities.

- Dual-Course Credit. Virginia should make sure that the American

History and Government course added to the public university General Education Requirements is also available as a dual credit course in public high schools. This dual credit course should possess rigorous standards, forbid Action Civics or activism, and have transparent syllabi.

- Reform Teaching Licensure. Education schools abuse their monopoly on teaching licensure to train teachers to teach social justice propaganda and Action Civics. States should establish teaching licensure pathways that allow teachers to avoid education schools and that establish a preference for subject-matter specialists over education majors. States should also require teachers in state public schools who teach English or Social Studies to pass six (6) survey courses in Western Heritage, American History, and American Government. These courses should include no Action Civics or activism.

We make these recommendations for a broad array of laws to institutionalize the prohibition of CRT, and to make sure it cannot return. We are aware, however, that education reformers do not yet possess a sure majority in Virginia's General Assembly. We urge Governor Youngkin and his administration to push for these laws both in hopes that they can secure immediate passage and to prepare the ground for legislation when a legislative majority can be secured.

We make these recommendations, and we make one further one of the utmost importance. Make sure the Virginia education bureaucracy enforces Executive Orders #1 and #2. Bureaucrats are past masters of the arts of noncompliance. We urge Governor Youngkin and his administration to make it a top priority that these Executive Orders actually go into effect, both in the state Education Department and in each public school district. We urge in particular that they take all necessary disciplinary measures to ensure that CRT advocates do not sabotage these reforms.

Governor Youngkin began his term very well. He will do even better by enforcing his Executive Orders. We urge him to ensure the long-term success of his agenda by passing a broad range of laws to institutionalize education reform.

With an Anti-Wokeness Platform

9 – Stopping America's Impending Destruction From Woke Madness

As we've seen and discovered through the chapters of this handbook, attempting to find any semblance of sapience in today's Progressive and woke arguments is as elusive as Big Foot, let alone facts, logic, and the truth. Furthermore, many Progressive policies are outright racist, unconstitutional, and Marxist based, at the very least. And finally, Progressives cannot admit they're wrong on so many issues, and continuously fail to produce logical arguments, provide proven results, and/or utilize unbiased data to back their ideology.

With so much going against today's Progressivism movement, the anti-Progressive long game must be focused on educational policies, legislation, and pedagogy that help wins the culture war by restoring conservative values, viewpoint diversity, and sapience to high school and college campuses—as well as enlighten their students, administrators, and faculty of the many blessings to humankind that are the direct result of Western European culture, American exceptionalism, and Judeo-Christian values.

This prudent approach, is a project of recapture and reinvention, enabling parents, independents, libertarians, and conservatives the opportunity to finally to demonstrate an effective countermeasures against Progressivism's long march through the institutions. The Progressive Left's permanent bureaucracy will be dead-set against this gambit, but if it succeeds, a new era for higher education—and for the country—is possible.

This task will be monumental, yet critical, to America's survival and future, and this chapter, along with the others, provides the means and methods to enable the mission and vision of concerned parents to reverse the idiocracy and hypocrisy of the woke and progressivist indoctrination of our children.

Outlined is essential information that every parent should know—as well as school board members who might be working with these parents or parents on a host of issues that this handbook covers. Who knows—one of them, or you, could end up running and winning a school board position.

Woke Schooling: A Toolkit for Concerned Parents

The Manhattan Institute offers an excellent "Woke Schooling: A Toolkit for Concerned Parents" toolkit that provides most everything concerned parents need to know about every aspect of defeating the Progressivism agenda at their woke schools. For a link to this toolkit, please check out the Appendix.

The following advice is based on conversations with a number of activists, journalists, and others who have spent the past several years pushing back on critical pedagogy in their children's and others' schools. It is not meant to be comprehensive but rather a starting point—a way for you to begin thinking about how you can take an active hand in making your child's school a better place for him or her to learn.

What follows are a few principles to keep in mind before taking action.

Proportionality

We are all probably aware of the most controversial instances of critical pedagogy in classrooms: the Buffalo, New York, school district that told students that they must become "activists for antiracism" instead of focusing on their failing test scores, or the California model "ethnic studies" curriculum that speaks approvingly of Aztec human sacrifice, to name just two cases. That these incidents made it into the national news means that they are rarefied examples of critical pedagogy at its most expansive.

By contrast, maybe the problem you are dealing with is a single assignment that your child's teacher has handed out—something that might have been hastily scraped from a seemingly reliable website. You could respond by calling down the school board or launching a boycott—but doing so may induce the board to circle the wagons and force a conflict where a few simple words would have made the problem evaporate.

But at times, you do need to prepare for an extended fight. When resolving any problem—including the problem of dangerous falsehoods in your child's classroom—it's important to make your response proportional to the scale of the issue. Throughout the rest of this section of the guide, we'll cover solutions ranging from a polite conversation to total parent boycott. Remember: start small and think about the scale of the problem before you go nuclear.

The Minority Rule

There is rarely such a thing as a truly popular movement, and the spread of critical pedagogy is no exception. Most diversity initiatives at major schools are spearheaded by administrators, often in a specifically designated department of diversity, equity, and inclusion (DEI); social media protests are often instigated by a small group of students or alumni, not a spontaneous and uncoordinated mass action.

The point is not about the legitimacy of these movements but about how they operate. A small group of people who demand something will generally get the compliance of the majority who are indifferent. This is what mathematician, investor, and social critic Nassim Taleb calls the "minority rule": the insight that majorities will follow minorities' preferences if the latter are intransigent and the former are "flexible."

This is a useful principle to understand not only because it allows you to focus on the minority of actors who are driving the change to which you object; it also makes you aware that you and other parents like you can together become an intransigent minority. If you're more stubborn than the most stubborn proponent of critical pedagogy in your school, you may win through intransigence alone.

Effective Persuasion

In every step of the process, it's important to keep in mind how you're communicating, which means keeping in mind with whom you're communicating. Your fundamental goal is a change at some level, whether it be in your child's classroom or across the whole school. To attain that change, you need to convince someone—a teacher, a principal, a school board—and therefore you need to think about effective persuasion.

In general, being polite and conciliatory is the correct first move—you catch more flies with honey than with vinegar. No one thinks of himself as a bad guy, including a teacher teaching your child something you don't want your child to learn. If you go in guns blazing, you are more likely to elicit a defensive response, which will move you further away from your goal. Do not allow politeness to make you a pushover—your goal should be calm and reasonable but firm.

That said, do not discount the effectiveness of getting angry, particularly if you find that you need to escalate past a one-on-one conversation. Advocates of critical pedagogy have wrung huge changes out of administrations through pressure campaigns built on assertions of "righteous rage" and "justified anger." The squeaky wheel, as it were, gets the grease, and you should not be afraid to match your opponents' level of being demanding—after all, it has been successful for them.

Another insight that can be gleaned from paying attention to critical pedagogy advocates: a story is worth a thousand arguments. The persuasiveness of so-called critical race stories comes from their pathos— anecdotes are a powerful tool for swaying public emotion, and you should actively strive to use them. You can outline why you think critical pedagogy is bad; but actual stories of how these practices are hurting kids are far more effective in changing the minds of administrators—never mind the community at large.

Solving the Problem Yourself

As mentioned, it's important to adapt your response to the scale of the problem. Before you do anything, assess the level at which the problem is happening. Although curricular guidelines may be set at the school district or even the state level, day-to-day decisions about what your children are reading and learning are still mostly in the hands of teachers. So start by consulting with their teachers: Is their use of a critical pedagogy resource a one-off, or is it part of a deliberate learning plan? Are they incorporating a variety of perspectives, or only offering one view? You may find that a simple conversation can get you further than you would have thought.

If the original teacher is recalcitrant, it's time to move up the administrative ladder. In a public school, that might mean the head of the division, the principal, and then the district superintendent's office. Be calm and polite but persistent—administrators should see you as someone who demands to be taken seriously. In a private school, that might mean going to the head of the division, followed by the head of the school.

While you're still prosecuting your issue on an individual level, here are a few tips to keep in mind:

Document everything. Make sure to save e-mails and take notes after meetings. Consider recording conversations—but be aware that this may be interpreted as hostile before you need to become hostile. If you do record conversations, be aware of the laws surrounding recording in your state.

Consider whether you want to press for your child to be able to opt out of the objectionable lesson/content. Such opt-outs have long existed—for example, for parents concerned about the content of sex education classes. Rather than asking your teacher/administrator to change the curriculum for everyone else, consider the pros and cons of keeping it away from your own child.

Don't let yourself be bullied. A major feature of critical pedagogy is the way that it dispatches critics through personal invective and guilt by association—dissenters are tarred as "racists," "white supremacists," and the like. You should recognize that these assertions are nothing more than an attempt to intimidate you; do not let these words have power over you. If you hold firm, the most ardent critical pedagogy advocates will quickly discover that they've run out of ammo.

Getting Organized

Maybe your efforts to address the problem one-on-one have gone nowhere, or maybe the problem was too big for a one-on-one solution. Some schools have implemented large-scale critical pedagogy programs, with the full endorsement of the administration and associated staff. In situations like that, your complaint about one teacher isn't going to cut it. What you need, then, is to move from solving the problem yourself to working in concert with other parents.

In fact, operating as a lone wolf may make it easier for the administration to dismiss your concerns. Be wary of techniques designed to mollify you without addressing the problem: for example, offering you a teacher's aide position, or a favored teacher for your child next year, or bringing in the PTA to outnumber you.

Your first step is to identify other parents who are sympathetic to your concerns and skeptical of the school's new direction. This is easier said than done—in a school that has fully leaned in to critical pedagogy, those who speak out critically may find themselves ostracized. You may need to be the first person to step forward by speaking out publicly, such as at a PTA meeting or over a parent e-mail list. Alternately, if you observe others expressing discontent or being reticent, approach them.

Another approach is to give parents an anonymous forum to vent, and then form connections. At Los Angeles's Harvard-Westlake School, an Instagram page called "Woke at Harvard-Westlake" has documented critical pedagogy excesses over the past year. It includes a public-facing e-mail address and form so that parents and students can contact its anonymous administrator(s). Such an anonymous venue could highlight absurdities in your school as well as help build connections.

A key reality of establishing a group of parents is that the bigger the group becomes, the easier it gets. That's because another parent you bring in might know two more sympathetic parents. But it's also because the bigger the group becomes, the easier it is to be comfortable affiliating with it— knowing that five other people are on your side is exponentially more comforting than knowing that only one person is.

After you have more than two or three parents on your side, it may make sense to create a central venue for coordination. An e-mail list works well, as does a group chat application like WhatsApp or Discord. For those who are particularly concerned about privacy, encrypted apps like Signal or Keybase may be a better option.

Being aware of other parents' privacy concerns is paramount to organizing a successful group. Particularly in private schools, where enrollment is at the discretion of the administration, parents might fear that dissenting from pedagogical practices will hurt their kids' educational future. Giving parents a variety of options to disclose information about themselves to you might be a useful way to build their confidence and trust—ultimately producing a more cohesive group. Encourage parents to engage anonymously in a text chat, and then encourage an in-person meeting when they seem comfortable doing so.

Responding as a Group

Once you've organized even a small group of parents, you want to think about how to make your voice heard at school. Consider a similar escalation strategy to the one outlined above in "Solving the Problem Yourself"—approach a problematic teacher, and if that proves futile, work your way up. In general, at this stage, you have two goals: the ultimate goal of correcting the problematic behavior; and the instrumental goal of attracting more parents to your cause.

You should consider the medium by which you and your group of parents communicate your displeasure. Parents at the Dalton School in New York, for example, penned an anonymous letter to the administration condemning the school's turn toward critical pedagogy; parents in the Southlake Public School District in Texas pushed through an entirely new school board. But you could also consider asking for a sit-down meeting before moving to that step. Remember the principle of proportionality: only escalate if your less aggressive response is not getting the desired results.

You should consider the trade-offs of anonymity. As mentioned, some parents will be uncomfortable attaching their names to any opposition to the school's "diversity" agenda, particularly if you are in a private school where your child has no formal right to attend. At the same time, anonymity is inherently delegitimizing: the Dalton letter gives no sense of how many or which parents are opposed to your school's critical pedagogy agenda. This gives opponents an opportunity to dismiss you as a small, irrelevant group—or as not confident enough of, or committed enough to, your views to defend them publicly. Be aware that at a certain point, anonymity will no longer be tenable.

Once you have tried direct conversation and accepted the need to go public, many responses become available. You could consider organizing your group to write letters to the editor of your local newspaper (more on this in the next section), attend your local PTA or school board meeting en masse, and even organize a real-life protest, as parents did after D.C.-area magnet high school Thomas Jefferson High School dumped its race-blind admissions test.

If you are a private school parent, now may also be a time to consider talking about annual contributions to the school, one of the few points of leverage that such parents have over their schools' administrations that advocates of critical pedagogy usually do not. A group of parents can inform their school that they will not be giving annual contributions if divisive material remains in the curriculum. Doing so connects the issue to the school's bottom line and may instigate change.

To the extent possible, it pays to be aware of the diversity of the people presenting criticism of an ideology that has framed itself, however dishonestly, as promoting diversity and inclusion. To the extent that parents from different racial/socioeconomic backgrounds are genuinely represented in your group, their public expression of criticism helps make the case that the group's concerns are not rooted in racism but in a genuine concern that "antiracism" may make discrimination worse, not better.

You also should consider offering a range of ways for parents to get involved, so that even those who don't want to do too much can do something. Make it easy to write a letter to your school board or principal by offering a form outlining the specific problem, alluding to more general objections to critical pedagogy, and emphasizing your investment as a parent in your child's right to an education that is free from racial and ethnic discrimination.

Similarly, if you write a letter to the editor of your local paper (see the next section on working with the media), you can then ask fellow parents to sign it, which is relatively easy for them but helps make their support for your project public.

Offering a Positive Vision

Pushing back against critical pedagogy is a worthwhile and noble project, but it is also important and helpful to be positive. Some people who support (or believe they support) critical pedagogy in schools have strange beliefs about critics, thinking, for example, that skeptical parents do not want their children to ever face hard historical truths, or that they support a whitewashing of American history. That's not the case: critics of critical pedagogy are concerned that it defines America in an exclusively and simplistically negative light, not that it offers any criticisms of America at all.

One solution to emphasize—particularly in history and social studies curricula at the middle-and high-school level—is the importance of presenting a variety of perspectives on an issue and trusting students to sort out right from wrong. Parents and administrators are likely to be far more open to adding thinkers to the curriculum than subtracting them—consider floating the works of moderate (and even left-leaning) academic critics of critical pedagogy like John McWhorter, Glenn Loury, Carol Swain, Erec Smith, Stephanie Deutsch, Peter Boghossian, and others.

A related strategy is to try to offset critical pedagogy's relentlessly negative account of ethnic relations with a more positive, affirmative story. Your student's school can use black history month to learn only about the "white supremacy" allegedly inherent in standardized tests or negative reactions to being called racist, or they can use it to celebrate great black Americans and try to respectfully build a better understanding of the many contributions of black people and black culture to America. Critical pedagogy's fixation on the negative can turn minority students into tokens of oppression—a more positive approach can help them celebrate who they are in school without dividing students into friend and foe.

Lastly, it is important to take seriously individual acts of bias and intolerance in schools. Regardless of critical pedagogy's claims, it's still the case that kids can be and often are cruel to each other—and parents should want an environment that minimizes and condemns bigoted bullying.

Adopting critical pedagogy training and "antiracist statements" actually lets school administrators avoid the much harder work of treating acts of bigotry as a disciplinary problem. If you want to push back on these practices, make clear that you agree that racism should not be tolerated in your school—but critical pedagogy is the wrong way to go about reducing it.

Working With the Media

If your parent-group actions aren't working, or even if they are, you might consider bringing public attention to the problem. Even if your child's school is united behind the idea of critical pedagogy, much of the nation is not. Bringing your story into the spotlight can apply much needed pressure, highlighting unreasonable behavior in a way that can fix it.

If you've been carefully documenting your activities until this point, those details will be invaluable. Other parents should have been doing so, as well. You may want to organize those details in a common Google Doc or other online file-sharing service.

If your child is enrolled in a public school, you might want to familiarize yourself with your state's freedom of information laws. As government entities, public schools are generally subject to such laws, and administrators can be compelled to release everything from internal documents to the texts of their e-mails. For a guide to your state's public records law, consult a group such as the National Freedom of Information Coalition.

Note that compelling the release of, say, a principal's e-mails is a very aggressive action—so do so only if you're prepared to burn bridges. But if your child is a public school student, freedom of information laws exist to help hold public employees accountable, so don't be afraid to use them. For example, investigative journalist Asra Nomani (whose son attends Virginia's public Thomas Jefferson High School) used her state's freedom of information law to reveal a $20,000 contract (for a one-hour video presentation) between Virginia's Fairfax County Public School district and critical race theorist Ibram X. Kendi.

Whether you want to publish your personal story, the details of other parents' struggles against the administration, or something that you've uncovered through a public records request, you need to think about the platform on which you do it. Self-publishing allows you to spread your message quickly without relying on others, but it also limits your reach (unless you already have a large social media following). By contrast, working with local—or national—outlets gives you a bigger platform but also reduces your control over the story.

If you'd like to self-publish, a wide variety of platforms are now available that are easy to set up and use.

Blogging services like Medium or WordPress allow you to set up a public-facing blog in minutes, while newsletter services like Substack enable you to produce similar output for a select list of subscribers. You might also consider using social media platforms like X (formerly Twitter) and Facebook to get the message out.

You can do only so much with such platforms, however, so you might want to approach the media. A good place to start is local media—your local paper or TV station—which are eager for local stories and, in general, less likely to be ideologically sympathetic to critical pedagogy than many large national outlets.

Before choosing to approach local media, consider whom you want to approach—a local television station, a local paper, etc. Take partisan slant into account—a right-leaning outlet will likely be more sympathetic but may give your opponents the opportunity to tar you as partisan yourself.

If you're not having success with the local media, or if you think that your message needs a broader audience, you might consider a news source with wider reach. A particularly clear-cut story of critical pedagogy–motivated wrongdoing may get traction at a national, left-leaning paper like the *New York Times* or *Washington Post*, but such outlets have evinced sympathy toward the goals of "antiracism," and thus might be less interested than you would hope.

Explicitly right-leaning outlets have the challenge of partisan tilt but are likely to be more sympathetic: consider sites like the Manhattan Institute's *City Journal*, *National Review*, *Epoch Times*, *Washington Examiner,* Daily Signal, local newspapers or Fox News station.

Working with such sites will be more likely to connect you to a journalist interested in your story but may also make it harder for your story to have an impact with other parents skeptical of these outlets. Last, consider particular angles of your story: if, for example, you are dealing with critical pedagogy–inspired antisemitism, a site like Tablet, which focuses on Jewish issues, may be interested.

Before you approach anyone in the media, organize the information you want to present—a PDF of the most salacious documents you can share, a list of other parents with whom they can talk, for example. Giving a journalist something to work with makes him or her much more likely to take your story.

When talking to a reporter, be aware of journalistic norms around quoting and attribution. Unless you have explicitly stipulated that the conversation is "off the record," and your interlocutor has agreed, assume that everything that you are saying can and will appear on the front page of your local newspaper tomorrow, and conduct yourself accordingly. Be courteous and avoid personal criticisms of your opponents—your problem is with a failure of teaching, not with the people you may be butting heads with.

The trade-off of going to the media is that while your story will get a wider audience, it also becomes no longer your story to control.

The journalist with whom you are working is free to quote you however he or she sees fit and is indeed professionally obligated to get the opinion of the "other side." This doesn't mean that you shouldn't approach the media, but you should be aware that your interlocutor's work product may not perfectly line up with how you imagined it.

While this guide advises speaking to the media only after you've tried internal recourse and sought to build connections to other parents, it's worth noting that a public story may have the effect of jump-starting those connections. Schools trying to push critical pedagogy over and above parents' objections have every reason to keep them in the dark and separated from each other, as many parents have experienced. A story about something crazy happening at your school can change the conversation, giving parents a concrete concern to discuss and coalesce around, and making the airing of thoughts socially permissible in a way that it previously was not.

Taking Legal Action

Critical pedagogy is not merely counterproductive and divisive, critics increasingly argue—it may also be illegal. The Fourteenth Amendment to the U.S. Constitution and the 1964 Civil Rights Act spell out certain rights to not be discriminated against on the basis of race, as well as certain guarantees of the right to free speech, even (in some cases) by students in public schools. Training and activities in public schools (and, potentially, private schools that have accepted federal funding) that divide students by race demean certain students as "oppressors" or inherently evil, or they compel students to profess certain beliefs that may run afoul of their state and federal rights.

These are the grounds for a number of lawsuits designed to fight back against critical pedagogy across the country. Although they are still in the early stages at the time of this guide's publication, they offer a promising approach for protecting students from discrimination, as well as a tool for you to consider when no other option is available.

Interested groups have, for example, sued the Santa Barbara Unified School District, the Democracy Prep Public Schools of Las Vegas, and Virginia's Thomas Jefferson High School. In these cases, plaintiffs have alleged that implicit bias training violates nondiscrimination rules, that compelled "antiracist" speech in the classroom is constitutionally impermissible, and that moves to end merit-based admissions to selective public high schools unconstitutionally discriminate against Asian-Americans.

Whether these arguments will be palatable to the courts remains to be seen. But parents should keep abreast of developments and consider whether their own situation could serve as a test case.

Whom Can I Ask for Help?

This guide is meant to be a starting point for parents looking to fight back against critical pedagogy in their school, but it's far from the only resource. Many national organizations—many brand-new—are interested in fighting various manifestations of critical pedagogy at every level of education, from kindergarten through college. They can help you connect to other parents, give you advice on organizing in your school, offer tips on talking to the media, and even help with lawsuits. Here are a few organizations:

Foundation Against Intolerance and Racism (see Appendix for link), a nonpartisan, centrist organization focused on responding to radicalism with a "compassionate anti-racism" dedicated to equal dignity and equality under the law. FAIR runs a membership organization, including local chapters, to help connect people from all parts of society skeptical of "woke" approaches that they term "neo-racism." It can also help connect parents like you to other parents and to professional and legal aid.

Foundation for Individual Rights and Expression (see Appendix for link), has historically focused on repressive speech policing at the college level, however, FIRE has been expanding its work to K–12 education. Its high school network offers a free-speech curriculum, as well as resources for parents and students concerned about their voices being silenced.

Pacific Legal Foundation (see Appendix for link), a national nonprofit public-interest law firm focusing on civil rights issues. It has recently taken an interest in critical pedagogy discrimination in public schools, organizing the lawsuit against Thomas Jefferson High School. If you are considering legal action, or if you believe that you have a test case, this organization may be a useful resource.

Parents Defending Education (see Appendix for link), a "national grassroots organization working to reclaim our schools from activists promoting harmful agendas," PDE is a school-focused group working to connect parents and provide resources to respond to critical pedagogy. It can help you find other parents in your local area and offer resources on how to respond effectively to your administration's agenda.

Conclusion

It's important not to make a mistake in thinking about politics simply in terms of a Left versus Right dynamic. That dynamic is significant, but where the opportunity really lies today is focusing on a top versus bottom dynamic.

An elite class, representing a small number of people with influence in the knowledge-based institutions, are acting in their own interest and against the interest of the vast majority of the American people—those who are still attached to the idea that America is a force for good and who think, to take just one example, that young children should be protected from the imposition of radical gender ideology.

In terms of the top versus bottom dynamic, the choice today is between the American Revolution of 1776 and the leftist revolution of the 1960s. The first offers a continued unfolding of America's founding principles of freedom and equality. The second ends up in nihilism and demoralization, just as the Weather Underground ended up in a bombed-out basement in Greenwich Village in the 1970s.

Even those of us who are temperamentally predisposed to defense must recognize that offense—laying siege to the institutions—is what is now demanded. Now is the time to become involved and get to work, saving America's destiny from Progressivism madness.

10 – The Moms for Liberty School Board Candidate Playbook & More

*Credit: Florida Today–Gov. Ron DeSantis is presented
"The Sword of Liberty" by Moms for Liberty co-founders
Tiffany Justice, left, and Tina Descovich, second from right
and executive director of program outreach Marie Rogerson during
the first Moms for Liberty National Summit on July 15, 2022 in Tampa.*

"I don't think parents should be telling schools what they should teach." Those were the famous words of Terry McAuliffe's failed 2021 gubernatorial campaign in Virginia.

The COVID-19 pandemic exposed just how little control parents have over their children's public school education. And their powerlessness did not end when many schools finally reopened their doors over a year into the pandemic. Parents across the nation still find themselves unable to access the materials used in their kids' public school curricula.

The deep chasm between the agendas of school board members and the interests of parents and their children has been exposed, and many parents are beginning to feel they must join the school boards themselves to make any real change in their children's education.

And that's exactly what they're doing. Parents with no experience working in the education system are running for and winning school board seats.

One such parent is Koleen Crawford of Londonderry, New Hampshire. Recognizing that remote learning during the pandemic resulted in significant learning loss for children, she laid out her reasons for running for a school board seat, stating, "I'm hoping to help bridge that gap to get our kids back to where they need to be academically."

Texas resident Scott Henry had never run for any sort of political office and had no political aspirations of any kind. In an interview with the *Washington Examiner,* Henry cited "the lack of transparency and accountability in our board" as the catalyst for his decision to run.

In addition to running for open seats, parents are attempting to recall school board members in record numbers. Even in leftist San Francisco, voters successfully recalled three incumbent school board members earlier this year after residents became frustrated with the board's priorities: renaming 44 schools and watering down the admissions process at one of its best high schools, all while running a $125 million deficit and keeping schools closed.

However, not all recall efforts have been successful—though the efforts themselves still send a powerful message.

New research from Michael Hartney of Boston College confirms and strengthens earlier findings that teachers unions "remain a potent force" in school board elections. In other work, Hartney says, "The important reality is that thousands of school board members will be 'elected' by tiny and unrepresentative electorates prior to next November's general election."

Teachers unions lobby school districts to hold elections off-cycle, that is, not at the same time as national elections. With many elections occurring in the spring or during odd years, most citizens who aren't union members aren't paying close attention and thus don't show up to vote.

As Sarah Anzia of the University of California, Berkeley, points out, "Members of interest groups with a large stake in an election outcome turn out at high rates regardless of election timing, and their efforts to mobilize and persuade voters have a greater impact when turnout is low."

Earlier research by Anzia confirms that not only do off-cycle elections decrease voter turnout, but they also lead to policy outcomes more favored by teachers unions.

This issue is widespread. Hartney's new research shows that "union favored candidates tend to win in both strong and weak union states and in conservative and liberal school districts." In the data collection at The Heritage Foundation, they counted only 15 states and the District of Columbia where all districts hold regular school board elections in November of even years—in other words, during regular election cycles where turnout is higher.

Until the emergence of Moms for Liberty, concerned parents were unlikely to consistently win elections for school boards with such a political process structured toward protecting existing organized interests. But this has changed now.

Whether it be private school, online curriculum, or private tutoring, the key component is that the people who know the student best are making the choices, not a teachers union or government bureaucrat. Parents have every right to be in control of their child's education. It's time for our education system to reflect that.

Moms for Liberty Leads the Way

This final section of the handbook is a brief introduction to America's premier and most powerful anti-woke school organization, Moms for Liberty (M4L). Moms for Liberty that has no equal, and they understand the importance of having liberty-minded school boards throughout the country that are focused on defending parental rights and improving education and they hope to activate these types of people to public service.

Moms for Liberty is dedicated to fighting for the survival of America by unifying, educating, and empowering parents to defend their parental rights at all levels of government. They activate liberty-minded leaders to serve in elected positions. Their members understand school board races are some of the most important elections on the ballot. Therefore, they seek to provide school board candidates with the resources to successfully run for office.

How Moms for Liberty Fights for Parent Rights:

- Promote Liberty – We hold decision makers accountable or we work to replace them with liberty-minded individuals.

- Spread Awareness – We spread awareness and an understanding of the limited role of government.

- Oppose Government Overreach – We stand together against government overreach and intimidation tactics.

- Promote Liberty – We promote teaching the principles of liberty in our homes and community.

- Engage on Key Issues – We engage our communities and elected leaders on key issues impacting our families.

- Activate to Public Service – We activate liberty-minded leaders to serve in elected positions.

In their own words:

Because this is an important way we fight for the survival of America, we have created a revolutionary Campaign Kit. The Kit empowers school board candidates to run and win by focusing on proven local-level campaign strategy that works. Most school board candidates are seeking office for the first time. Using our Campaign Kit, they can come to understand campaign cycles, perfect voter communication, and avoid the common pitfalls that tend to trip up new candidates.

The Candidate Handbook covers:

Campaign cycles, your campaign team, knowing your numbers, getting out the vote, fundraising, voter contact, messaging, and more!

The Campaign Workbook facilitates:

Setting fundraising, canvassing, and vote goals. Crafting budgets, platforms, and talking points. As well as tracking volunteers, timelines, and more!

The Collateral Collection includes:

Templates to create campaign logos, yard signs, palm cards, mailers, postcards, and more!

Whether you win or lose your school board race, the battle continues!

If you win your race, you are likely to receive an invitation from your state's School Board Association offering to train you. Many of these Associations foster the same woke propaganda Moms for Liberty is fighting against. Instead, consider seeking training from groups that align with your values.

The Leadership Institute has a New School Board Member Training Program. This course arms newly elected school board members with the knowledge and abilities needed to manage their district successfully. This training will benefit both newly elected and current conservative school board members, as well as school board candidates and active citizens. Reach out to them for a copy at their link in the Appendix.

If you run and the results don't go your way, you can still have a positive impact on your community's children by establishing a Moms for Liberty chapter and advocating for changes you would like to see. See the Appendix to learn more about starting a Chapter of Moms for Liberty!

The Moms for Liberty Campaign Kit for First-Time Candidates

A year ahead of the 2024 election, Moms for Liberty announced the release of a campaign kit for school board candidates in September 2023, saying they had endorsed more than 500 board campaigns last year and drawn from what they learned then.

Moms for Liberty, founded in 2021 by Descovich and Justice, is a conservative group pushing for parental rights in public education, with a focus on topics including COVID-19 restrictions, critical race theory, LGBTQ issues and removing what they believe to be inappropriate material from school libraries. The group has gained national attention for its members' protests at school board meetings and efforts to remove books from school libraries.

Since Moms for Liberty was founded, it has grown to include 300 chapters in 47 states with more than 130,000 members.

"We are revolutionizing school board campaigns," Marie Rogerson said in a September 2023 press release. Rogerson, executive director of program development for Moms for Liberty, added that more than half of the first-time candidates the conservative parents group endorsed in 2022 won.

"With this innovative new Campaign Kit, candidates can avoid the pitfalls that tend to trip up first-time candidates."

In their announcement, Moms for Liberty members said their Campaign Kit would help prepare first-time candidates for office. The kit includes a candidate handbook, which members describe as a "how to" guide on how to run for school board; a workbook with resources for creating an effective campaign plan; and a collateral collection with design templates for logos, mailers and more.

In a joint statement in the release, founders Tina Descovich and Tiffany Justice said as former school board members from Brevard and Indian River County, Florida, they'd both received numerous questions on how to run a successful campaign.

"This candidate tool kit is going to be a game changer," they said in the statement. "We are proud to provide this tool kit for candidates to have their questions answered while also learning how to run an effective campaign. We are excited to empower liberty minded individuals who want to make a difference in their communities and in their schools."

The kit is free for Moms for Liberty members on their website. See the Appendix for Moms for Liberty website link and membership signup, plus more.

Moms for Liberty Co-founder Tina Descovich Appointed to Florida Commission on Ethics

Gov. Ron DeSantis announced in September 2023 the appointment of Moms for Liberty co-founder and former Brevard County school board member Tina Descovich to Florida's Commission on Ethics. Tina Descovich co-founded the organization in 2021.

Descovich, who served on Brevard's school board from 2016 to 2020, founded Moms for Liberty with former Indian River school board member Tiffany Justice in 2021. The group has been outspoken about topics including COVID-19 restrictions, critical race theory, LGBTQ issues and removing what they view as inappropriate material from school libraries. The group has garnered national attention for its members' protests at school board meetings and efforts to remove books from school libraries.

In a text to *Florida Today*, Descovich said she was honored to be appointed to the commission.

"The Florida Ethics Commission is charged with serving as the guardian of the standards of conduct for public officers and employees as well as safeguarding public trust," she said. "It will be a privilege to serve the state I love as a member of this commission."

Since it was founded, the organization—which was labeled an extremist group by ultra-left Southern Poverty Law Center in June—has grown to include 299 chapters in 46 states with more than 130,000 members. Their second annual "Joyful Warriors" summit was held at the end of June 2023 in Philadelphia, with speakers including presidential candidates Donald Trump, Ron DeSantis, Nikki Haley and Vivek Ramaswamy.

The Commission on Ethics lost its chairperson near the end of August, when Glen Gilzean Jr. resigned, choosing instead to keep his job as Disney district administrator with the Central Florida Tourism Oversight District and the $400,000 salary that came with it.

Members of the commission are not allowed to hold any public employment, though Gilzean said he was unaware of a possible conflict.

Prior to forming Moms for Liberty, Descovich was elected to Brevard's school board in 2016, where she served until she lost the seat to Jennifer Jenkins in the 2020 election. In 2018, she was chosen to serve as president of the Florida Coalition of School Board Members, which at the time described itself as a nonpartisan alternative to the Florida School Boards Association.

Descovich was appointed to the Commission on Ethics alongside Luis Fuste, an attorney from Miami. Both appointments must be confirmed by the Florida Senate.

The Heritage Foundation Fight For Parental Rights In Education

The Heritage Foundation is working with Heritage Action for America to protect parents' rights, fight back against dangerous left-wing agendas infiltrating schools, and partner with parents and allies at the state and local level to advance much-needed education reforms.

Heritage Action for America, more commonly known simply as Heritage Action, is a conservative policy advocacy organization founded in 2010. Heritage Action, which has affiliates throughout the United States, is a sister organization of the conservative think tank The Heritage Foundation

Heritage Action, with two million grassroots activists, hosted its first Save Our Schools Parental Rights Symposium on June 23, 2023 in Dana Point, California. The event highlighted how Heritage Action is working alongside parents to protect their rights over their children's education. Over 100 concerned parents plus education advocates, grassroots leaders, and Heritage Action staff came together to fight back against the dangerous agendas infiltrating public schools.

Heritage Action Executive Director Jessica Anderson spoke about the critical purpose of the event:

"The education system has long been a tool for the far left to indoctrinate children with their radical political agenda. Now, as school boards, teachers unions, and elected officials try to take parents out of their children's education and force woke curriculum on our children, parents need to know how to most effectively fight back.

"These Parental Rights Symposiums are just one part of Heritage Action's efforts to restore parents' rights and save our schools. Through training parents on how to run for school board, speak up at local meetings, advocate for school choice policy, and stay involved with their children's curriculum, our grassroots activists will have the tools necessary to advance much needed education reforms."

The event opened with a panel discussion featuring Jonathan Butcher, Will Skillman Fellow in Education Policy at The Heritage Foundation, and Merianne Jensen, a concerned mother and education advocate. The Heritage Foundation has been providing recommendations for much-needed education reforms at the state and federal levels, and the panel focused on how allies at the state and local level can work to advance those reforms.

The event also included training sessions on how to run for your local school board, how to help maintain election integrity in the face of efforts to change election laws to make it easier to commit fraud, and how to stay engaged in your child's education and hold schools accountable.

Following the training sessions, guests were given the opportunity to talk with the speakers and other attendees and also hear from Kari Lake, former Fox Anchor and education grassroots leader. Virginia Attorney General Jason Miyares gave the keynote speech over dinner, stressing the importance of parental involvement in education. Jonathan Isaac, professional basketball player and author of Why I Stand, closed by sharing his inspiring thoughts on why it's so important to stand up for what you believe in, especially when standing up for those who can't necessarily stand up for themselves.

In August, Heritage Action will hold a second Parental Rights Symposium in Virginia Beach, Virginia. In addition to these symposiums and lobbying efforts for several education bills in states across the country, Heritage Action also launched SaveOurSchools.com, a one-stop shop of resources for parents interested in engaging with their children's school system.

More Parental Rights Resources

The Heritage Foundation and other think tanks have partnered with congruent organizations to provide various model legislation, including their own, that states and their school boards can use to protect education freedom. For more information about the resources below, please check out the Appendix for their websites.

Academic Transparency Act - Goldwater Institute

Ballotpedia:
- School Board Elections – 2023
- School Board Elections – 2024

Beyond Red vs. Blue: The Political Typology - 11. Progressive Left - Pew Research

Candidate Handbook - Moms for Liberty

Censorship and the First Amendment in Schools - A Resource Guide

Civic Literacy Act - American Legislative Exchange Council (ALEC)

Critical Race Theory Briefing Book

Foundation Against Intolerance and Racism (FAIR)

Foundation for Individual Rights and Expression (F.I.R.E.)

Free Speech Alliance - Media Research Center (MRC)

Goldwater Institute - Academic Transparency Act

Heritage Foundation, The:
- Heritage Action for America (Heritage Action)
- Model School Board Policy on Parental Rights in Education and Safety, Privacy, and Respect for All Students in the District
- Protecting K–12 Students from Discrimination
- The Given Name Act
- School Board Training
- Education Freedom Report Card
- Protecting Children and Families with Parents' Bills of Rights

- Save Our Schools Model Legislation
- The Critical Classroom

Institute for Justice:
- Education Savings Account Act: Publicly Funded
- Education Savings Account Act: Tax-Credit Funded

K-12 Code of Ethics

Leadership Institute:
- New School Board Member Training Program
- School Board Leadership

Manhattan Institute:
- How to Regulate Critical Race Theory in Schools
- Abolish DEI Bureaucracies and Restore Colorblind Equality in Public Universities
- Woke Schooling – A Toolkit for Concerned Parents
- A Model for School Practices Relating to Sexuality and Gender
- A Model for Transparency in School Training and Curriculum Gender

Pacific Legal Foundation

Parent Revolt - California GOP (CAGOP)

Parents Defending Education

Parent Union:
- Parental Rights Pledge
- How to Track Political Contributions
- How to Hold Your School Board Accountable

Safe Libraries

The Joy of Being Wrong (Video)

The Women's Bill of Rights - Independent Women's Voice

.

Appendix

Academic Transparency Act - Goldwater Institute:
https://www.goldwaterinstitute.org/wp-content/uploads/2022/07/Academic-Transparency-Act-2022-Model-Legislation-6-22.pdf.

BALLOTPEDIA:
- **School Board Elections – 2023:**
  https://ballotpedia.org/School_board_elections,_2023.

- **School Board Elections – 2024:**
  https://ballotpedia.org/School_board_elections,_2024.

Beyond Red vs. Blue: The Political Typology - 11. Progressive Left - Pew Research Center: https://www.pewresearch.org/politics/2021/11/09/progressive-left/.

Candidate Handbook - Moms for Liberty:
https://www.momsforliberty.org/about/.

Censorship and the First Amendment in Schools – A Resource Guide - National Coalition Against Censorship:
https://www.webjunction.org/documents/webjunction/Censorship_in_Schools_Learning_Speaking_and_Thinking_Freely_The_First_Amendment_in_Schools.html.

Civic Literacy Act - American Legislative Exchange Council (ALEC).
www.alec.org/model-policy/the-civic-literacy-act/.

Critical Race Theory Briefing Book: https://cplaction.com/wp-content/uploads/CRT-Briefing-Book-Rufo.pdf.

Foundation Against Intolerance and Racism (FAIR): https://www.fairforall.org.

Foundation for Individual Rights and Expression (F.I.R.E.):
https://www.thefire.org.

Free Speech Alliance - Media Research Center (MRC).
https://www.mrc.org/freespeechalliance.

HERITAGE FOUNDATION, THE:
- **Heritage Action for America (Heritage Action):** https://heritageaction.com/.

- **Education Freedom Report Card:** https://www.heritage.org/educationreportcard/index.html.

- **Model School Board Policy on Parental Rights in Education and Safety, Privacy, and Respect for All Students in the District:** https://www.heritage.org/model-school-board-policy-parental-rights-education-and-safety-privacy-and-respect.

- **Protecting Children and Families with Parents' Bills of Rights:** https://www.heritage.org/education/report/protecting-children-and-families-parents-bills-rights.

- **Protecting K–12 Students from Discrimination:** https://www.heritage.org/protecting-k-12-students-discrimination.

- **Save Our Schools Model Legislation:** https://saveourschools.com/model-legislation

- **School Board Training:** https://www.heritage.org/school-board-training.

- **The Given Name Act**: https://www.heritage.org/the-given-name-act.

INSTITUTE FOR JUSTICE:
- **Education Savings Account Act: Publicly Funded:** https://ij.org/legislation/education-savings-account-act-publicly-funded/.

- **Education Savings Account Act: Tax-Credit Funded:** https://ij.org/legislation/education-savings-account-act-tax-credit-funded/.

K-12 Code of Ethics – Freedom Center On Campus: https://www.freedomcenteroncampus.org/k-12-code-of-ethics/#comment-45056.

LEADERSHIP INSTITUTE:
- **New School Board Member Training Program:** https://www.leadershipinstitute.training/courses/new-school-board-member .

- **School Board Leadership:** https://www.leadershipinstitute.training/courses/school-board-leadership.

MANHATTAN INSTITUTE:

- **A Model for School Practices Relating to Sexuality and Gender:** https://manhattan.institute/article/a-model-for-school-practices-relating-to-sexuality-and-gender.

- **A Model for Transparency in School Training and Curriculum Gender:** https://manhattan.institute/article/a-model-for-transparency-in-school-training-and-curriculum.

- **Abolish DEI Bureaucracies and Restore Colorblind Equality in Public Universities:** https://media4.manhattan-institute.org/sites/default/files/model_dei_legislation013023.pdf.

- **How to Regulate Critical Race Theory in Schools: A Primer and Model Legislation:** https://media4.manhattan-institute.org/sites/default/files/copland-crt-legislation.pdf.

- **The Critical Classroom:** The Heritage Foundation. https://www.heritage.org/the-critical-classroom.

- **Woke Schooling – A Toolkit for Concerned Parents:** https://www.manhattan-institute.org/woke-schooling-toolkit-for-concerned-parents.

Pacific Legal Foundation: https://www.pacificlegal.org

Parent Revolt - California GOP (CAGOP): https://www.cagop.org/s/parentrevolt.

Parents Defending Education: https://www.defendinged.org

PARENT UNION:

- **How to Hold Your School Board Accountable:** https://www.parentunion.org/toolkits-1/school-accountability.

- **How to Research School Performance:** https://www.parentunion.org/toolkits-1/school-performance.

- **How to Track Political Contributions:** https://www.parentunion.org/toolkits-1/political-donations.

- **Parental Rights Pledge:** Pdf Version at https://californiapolicycenter.org/wp-content/uploads/2023/08/Parental-Rights-Pledge.pdf or Sign the Pledge Version at https://docs.google.com/forms/d/e/1FAIpQLScoKe32NqJbQxAUr0S-EKA51ZYZHn5pTHvkhKJGfrFD1Pptrg/viewform?pli=1.

Pennsbury School Board Aggressive Censorship of CRT Debate:
https://www.ifs.org/wp-content/uploads/2021/10/PennsburySchoolBoard.mp4

Safe Libraries: https://safelibraries.blogspot.com/p/about-me.html.

The Joy of Being Wrong (Video): John Templeton Foundation.
https://youtu.be/mRXNUx4cua0.

The Women's Bill of Rights - Independent Women's Voice:
https://womensliberationfront.org/news/iwv-wolf-womens-bill-of-rights.

References

Beienburg, Matt. "Judge roasts teachers union hysterics over Florida curriculum transparency." Fox News. August 8, 2023. https://www.foxnews.com/opinion/judge-roasts-teachers-union-hysterics-over-florida-curriculum-transparency.

Cai, Jinghong. "The Public's Voice: Uncontested Candidates and Low Voter Turnout Are Concerns in Board Elections." National School Boards Association. April 1, 2020. https://www.nsba.org/ASBJ/2020/April/the-publics-voice.

Copland, James R., John Ketcham and Christopher F. Rufo. "Next Step for the Parents' Movement: Curriculum Transparency." *City Journal.* December 1, 2021. https://www.city-journal.org/how-to-achieve-transparency-in-schools.

Kennedy, Dana. "Librarians go radical as new woke policies take over: experts." *New York Post.* Sep. 10, 2022. https://nypost.com/2022/09/10/librarians-go-radical-as-new-woke-policies-take-over-experts/.

Hartney, Michael. "Schooled by DeSantis." *City Journal.* November 15, 2022. https://www.city-journal.org/ron-desantis-school-board-candidates-vs-teachers-unions.

Heritage and Heritage Action Fight For Parental Rights In Education. June 24, 2022. https://www.heritage.org/education/impact/heritage-and-heritage-action-fight-parental-rights-education.

Hochman, Nate. "The Parents' Revolt." *City Journal.* Autumn 2022. https://www.city-journal.org/article/the-parents-revolt.

Izumi, Lance, Wenyuan Wu and McKenzie Richards. *The Great Parent Revolt: How Parents and Grassroots Leaders Are Fighting Critical Race Theory in America's Schools.* Pacific Research Institute. Pasadena, CA. 2022.

Jilani, Zaid. "Progressives Against Transparency." *City Journal.* January 26, 2022. https://www.city-journal.org/progressives-against-school-transparency.

Mansfield, Erin and Kayla Jimenez. "These PACS are funding 'parents' rights advocates running for local school board positions." *USA Today.* October 2022 https://www.yahoo.com/entertainment/pacs-funding-parents-rights-advocates-100017559.html.

Nickels, Thom. "No Cause for Controversy." *City Journal.* May 6, 2022. https://www.city-journal.org/florida-parental-rights-law-should-be-no-cause-for-controversy.

Parental Rights Are Not 'Dangerous.' Goldwater Institute. September 12, 2023. https://www.goldwaterinstitute.org/parental-rights-are-not-dangerous/?gclid=CjwKCAjwvfmoBhAwEiwAG2tqzAN06rCXPZS10IIkII1pCAJMKvT-lanO7WaoJkMQkueP_jIK_dvBSRoCqkEQAvD_BwE.

Randall, David. "Gov. Youngkin Bans Critical Race Theory, but More Reform is Necessary." National Association of Scholars. January 18, 2022. https://www.nas.org/blogs/article/gov-youngkin-bans-critical-race-theory-but-more-reform-is-necessary.

Roberts, Ph.D., Kevin D. "Parents' Bill of Rights Is How Congress Can Help State School Reformers." Mar. 24, 2023. https://www.heritage.org/education/commentary/parents-bill-rights-how-congress-can-help-state-school-reformers.

Rufo, Christopher F. "How to Combat Gender Theory in Public Schools." *City Journal.* Feb. 07 2023. https://www.city-journal.org/article/how-to-combat-gender-theory-in-public-schools.

Rufo, Christopher F. "The Courage of Our Convictions." *City Journal.* April 22, 2021. https://www.city-journal.org/how-to-fight-critical-race-theory.

Rufo, Christopher F. "The Fight for Curriculum Transparency." *City Journal.* February 23, 2022. https://www.city-journal.org/the-fight-for-curriculum-transparency.

Salzman, Philip Carl. "Hate and Fear Are Now Major Motivators on Campus." *Epoch Times.* October 11, 2022. https://www.theepochtimes.com/hate-and-fear-are-now-major-motivators-on-campus_4785439.html?utm_medium=search&utm_source=ai.

Salzman, Philip Carl. "National Suicide by Education." Minding the Campus. September 23, 2022. https://www.mindingthecampus.org/2022/09/23/national-suicide-by-education/.

Salzman, Philip Carl. "Safeguarding Our Republic From Progressivism Madness." *Epoch Times.* October 11, 2022. https://www.theepochtimes.com/hate-and-fear-are-now-major-motivators-on-campus_4785439.html?utm_medium=search&utm_source=ai.

Sand, Larry. "School Transparency Wars." Education Reform. March 4, 2022. https://californiapolicycenter.org/school-transparency-wars/.

Sand, Larry. "What School Shutdowns Have Wrought." *City Journal*. March 16, 2021. https://www.city-journal.org/what-school-shutdowns-have-wrought.

Schalin, Jay. "The Pushback Against Classroom Indoctrination Begins." The James G. Martin Center for Academic Renewal. July 20, 2022. https://www.jamesgmartin.center/2022/07/the-pushback-against-classroom-indoctrination-begins/.

Schoof, John and Benjamin Tardif. The Heritage Foundation. "Political Deck Stacked Against Parents Running for School Board." Apr. 12, 2022. https://www.heritage.org/education/commentary/political-deck-stacked-against-parents-running-school-board.

Seminara, Dave. "The Left Twists the Meaning of 'Book Ban.'" *City Journal*. Jun. 26 2023. https://www.city-journal.org/article/the-left-twists-the-meaning-of-book-ban.

Sofield, Tom. "Pennsbury Settles First Amendment Lawsuit For $300,000." LevittownNow.com. July 15, 2022. https://levittownnow.com/2022/07/15/pennsbury-settles-first-amendment-lawsuit-for-300000/.

Swanson, Sheridan. "Critical Race Theory: Its Origins and Infiltration of California Public Schools.: California Policy Center (CPC). 2023. https://californiapolicycenter.org/reports/critical-race-theory-its-origins-and-infiltration-of-californias-public-schools/.

Tolson, Patricia. "Statistics Show America's Education System is Failing: CRT and Lower Expectation Equals Fewer Literate Graduates, Expert Says." *Epoch Times*. January 2, 2022. https://www.theepochtimes.com/statistics-show-americas-education-system-is-failing-crt-and-lower-expectation-equals-fewer-literate-graduates-expert-says_4179014.html.

Walker, Finch. "The Moms for Liberty Campaign Kit for First-Time Candidates." *Florida Today*. Sep. 20, 2023. https://www.floridatoday.com/story/news/2023/09/20/campaign-kit-for-school-board-candidates-released-by-moms-for-liberty/70901966007/.

Walker, Finch. "Moms for Liberty Co-founder Tina Descovich Appointed to Florida Commission on Ethics." *Florida Today*. Sep. 6, 2023. https://www.floridatoday.com/story/news/2023/09/06/desantis-appoints-moms-for-liberty-co-founder-to-ethics-commission/70776375007/.

Walsh, Mark. "What Do 'Parents' Rights' Mean Legally for Schools, Anyway?" Education Week. October 20, 2022. https://www.edweek.org/policy-politics/what-do-parents-rights-mean-legally-for-schools-anyway/2022/10.

Weissmueller, Zach. "Florida Parents Take Back the Classroom." Reason. January 28, 2022. https://reason.com/video/2022/01/28/florida-parents-take-back-the-classroom/.

Weslander Quaid, Michele R. "We Are in a War for America's Soul." *Epoch Times*. September 21, 2021. https://www.theepochtimes.com/we-are-in-a-war-for-americas-soul_4001263.html?utm_source=ai_recommender&utm_medium=a_bottom_above_etv.

Whitehead, Beth "With Nebraska Group's Withdrawal, Half of the 50 States Have Now Ditched the NSBA for Targeting Parents." The Federalist. June 15, 2022. https://thefederalist.com/2022/06/15/with-nebraska-groups-withdrawal-half-of-the-50-states-have-now-ditched-the-nsba-for-targeting-parents/.

Index

With an Anti-Wokeness Platform

Author Bio

Corey Lee Wilson

Corey Lee Wilson was raised an atheist by his liberal *Playboy* Bunny mother, has three Anglo-Hispanic siblings, a bi-racial daughter, a brother who died of AIDS, baptized a Protestant by his conservative grandparents, attended temple with his Jewish foster parents, baptized again as a Catholic for his first Filipina wife, attends Buddhist ceremonies with his second Thai wife, became an agnostic on his own free will for most of his life, and is a lifetime independent voter.

Corey felt the sting of intellectual humility by repeating the 4th grade and attended eighteen different schools (17 in California and one in the Bahamas) before putting himself through college (without parents) at Mt. San Antonio College and Cal Poly Pomona University (while on triple secret probation).

Named Who's Who of American College Students in 1984, he received a BS in Economics (summa cum laude) and won his fraternity's most prestigious undergraduate honor, the Phi Kappa Tau Fraternity's Shideler Award, both in 1985. In 2020, he became a member of the Heterodox Academy, in 2021 a member of the National Association of Scholars and 1776 Unites, and in 2023 became a member of Moms for Liberty.

As a satirist and fraternity man, Corey started Fratire Publishing in 2012 and transformed the fiction "fratire" genre to a respectable and viewpoint diverse non-fiction genre promoting practical knowledge and wisdom to help everyday people navigate safely through the many hazards of life. In 2019, he founded the S.A.P.I.E.N.T. Being to help promote freedom of speech, viewpoint diversity, intellectual humility and most importantly advance sapience in America's students and campuses.

Some readers might be prone to ask why would someone raised as a wild-hippy-gypsy child of the Sixties take the conservative path and champion conservative causes?

Quick answer: In this day and age it's the reasonable, logical, and sapient thing to do. By comparison, there is nothing "sapient" about the Progressivism movement and the woke madness that follows it throughout our educational systems.

Furthermore, to quote Ronald Reagan, "There's a flickering spark in us all which, if struck at just the right age, can light the rest of our lives." His spark was ignited in college when he experienced first-hand in the early Eighties the growing illiberalism at his college newspaper and its persistent bias against conservatives, Christians, and President Reagan.

Hopefully, this *Winning School Board Elections* guide will do the same to spark your inspiration and help you craft your anti-wokeness platform and winning strategy for your school board election.